What People Are Saying About *Successful Sex*

"While working directly with Laurie for seventeen years, I have seen firsthand her ability to put couples at ease with her straightforward yet sensitive style. This book reflects this and is extremely valuable for any couple."

— Brooke Schoppmann, MA

"This book is very informative without being uncomfortable. Laurie makes it interesting, and the fact that it is short and covers all the points needed makes it a really unique book! I can see any young couple especially benefiting from this book."

— Haley Bettridge, a twenty-six-year-old wife

"I work with premarital couples as well as high-conflict married couples. This valuable book has clear, direct information that I wish that I had thirty years ago (at the beginning of my career), when I first began giving couples remarriage and marriage counseling. The information is clear, direct, and most often hidden from those that need it most.

This valuable short read will be fodder for thousands of

excellent conversations that couples are required to engage in if they are to be happily married. It is timely informa-tion that I will refer my clients to from all of my clinics."

— Matt Eschler, PhD, LMFT

"I LOVED the book! It was very easy to read, very infor-mational without being graphic, and didn't take long to read. This is a great book for new and experienced cou-ples alike."

— Cody Dirks, a twenty-two-year-old fiancé

"Successful Sex is a remarkably refreshing introduction to the first sexual encounter as a married couple. It gives a much-needed positive view of this most important 'first time' and beyond for couples, to launch them on a success-ful and joyful marital journey of intimacy."

— Julie O'Neill King,
CNM with over twenty years of helping women

"I read this book right before I got married. So glad I did! It's a concise, quick read and teaches you things about inti-macy that I'd never previously thought of! Very informative and helpful."

— Chet Higby, a twenty-one-year-old husband

SUCCESSFUL
SEX

For the Virginal, Newlywed, or Experienced Couple

A Respectful, Essential, and Concise Guide to Sexual
Pleasure Together

S. LAURIE HANSEN, CNM

Publishing support provided by
Ignite Press
5070 N. Sixth St. #189
Fresno, CA 93710
www.IgnitePress.us

ISBN: 979-8-9860615-0-4
ISBN: 979-8-9860615-1-1 (E-book)

Should you desire to purchase this book for patient or classroom educational purposes, gift purposes, or congregational purposes, quantity discounts are available. Special pamphlets or a book excerpt can be created for you if you have a specific need. For more information, please contact:

Laurie Hansen
SuccessfulBookSeries@gmail.com

Because of the dynamic nature of the Internet, web addresses or links contained in this book may have been changed since publication and may no longer be valid.

The express purpose of this book is solely for information and education. No portion of this book is intended to replace treatment by a practicing medical provider.

The author has used her own personal and medical knowledge and experiences as the sources of information for the writing of this book. Names in the stories have been changed when needed, and permission has been obtained from involved persons when applicable. Any slights of people, places, or organizations are unintentional.

Library of Congress Control Number: 2022905921

Cover design by Lindsey Petersen
Edited by Emma Hatcher
Interior design by Eswari Kamireddy

FIRST EDITION

F1

To my grandchildren and all of the incredible youth in the world.
May their lives be filled with honesty and love.

THANKS

Thanks to all of the women I have been privileged to learn from—for sharing with me and for blessing me with your own, precious life experiences.

Thanks also to my husband, Jeff, as well as my daughters, my sons-in-law, my friends, and my colleagues for their honest feedback and support.

CONTENTS

INTRODUCTION

Most women and men eagerly await their first sexual encounter and look forward to this most precious time together. They do not need much guidance because of their passion and inherent instincts. However, the simple pearls in this book can help them sidestep common errors found in many sexual relationships. I specifically address the virginal couple in my introduction because of the unique way I approach this subject with some extra helps for them. However, my straightforward but respectful approach to the issue of sexual pleasure together is beneficial to all.

Some couples choose to wait to consummate their marriage on their wedding night for various reasons. This practice can be foreign to much of our society today. If a couple has avoided any premarital sexual activity, there may be a need for education about their bodies and sexual health. However, if a couple perceives that the education provider isn't respectful or doesn't understand or honor their decision for sexual abstinence, they may shy away from obtaining that information and help.

I believe that God meant for us to enjoy sex as a vital part of marriage. This positive approach has encouraged couples with similar beliefs (plus others without those beliefs) to seek me out because of the respect that I give the subject. This, together with my vast number of years of experience and medical knowledge, allows me to counsel and teach in an extremely effective style that feels safe, nonjudgmental, and approachable.

The information in this book is not discussed in most clinics, homes, or books. When I have attended medical conferences in other parts of the country, and I mention the *premarital appointment*, some of the medical providers attending the conference are surprised that I have virginal couples getting married. They don't see a need for this type of appointment and have stated that couples can work it out in the backseat of a car. But even if you have had sex zero times, one time, or many times, it doesn't mean that you have gained the awareness of what you need for a healthy and prospering sexual relationship in marriage. If I could count the couples who have thanked me for helping them achieve sexual satisfaction in their marriage, you would know it has been worth every bit of the extra time that I have spent during these appointments.

1

WHY THIS BOOK?

At nineteen years old, I was pretty much all alone in the musty college office—or so I thought. The history professor had piled clutters of books and papers in various places. Still, I had carved out an area where I typed away, using the old, black manual typewriter. My job was to type up his lectures.

I opened the door into the indoor hallway; it was my attempt to let in some air. Startled at seeing a forty-year-old man—who was clean-shaven but old-fashioned looking—I jumped just a bit, asking nervously, "Can I help you with something?" He was sitting uncomfortably on the floor directly across the hall, outside the door to another office. After he answered that he had an appointment with the neighboring professor, I left him alone.

After about thirty minutes, no one showed up to his appointment. Upon my offering him a chair, he volunteered that he was an army recruiter for the US Army Reserve 449th Petroleum Company. Being naïve and unaware of what an army recruiter does, I mentioned that I had a friend in the army reserve who was making $55 a weekend (which was a lot of money when the minimum wage was only $1.65 per hour). My father had died in a car wreck a month before, and I'd also lost my mother when I was fourteen years old. I had no one to guide me in my decisions. As I said earlier, I was pretty much all alone.

Though I was a student nurse at the time, and joining a medical unit would have been more beneficial for me, he never offered that information to me, so I didn't know that it was even an option. He instead sold me on his unit, the 449th, as that was how army recruiters made their money. Before realizing what was happening, there I was in green fatigues, sitting in a large army barrack on a Saturday morning with about one hundred men. We attended drill one weekend a month, and there were only three or four females in the entire company. We did a lot of sitting around or driving and, throughout all of it, talking.

During these times, I would listen to the "man talk." Men would often complain about their wives not wanting or liking sex. Some complained that they would bring home pretty, negligee underwear for her to wear, and she would never use it. Others said that their wives never wanted to do anything fun anymore. They expressed that their wives only wanted to talk about the kids and money, which the men felt was a distraction from their sexual relationship. Many were discouraged about their marriages.

I was uncomfortable during these personal revelations from this group of men I barely knew. With my inexperience, it was hard to understand how to respond, and I felt sorry for them and their wives. I remember thinking that I would be so hurt if I had a future husband that talked about me or our marriage like that to anyone. If I could help it, my husband would never need to express himself to anyone in that way.

After I was married to my late husband, Greg, I graduated and started working as a registered nurse in labor and delivery at the local hospital. My girlfriends and women at work would "girl talk." Though some women had a great love and desire for sex, others complained that they were dissatisfied with their sex life and that their husbands never spent time talking with them anymore. Some expressed that all that their husbands would do was go to work, come home, dump their shoes on the floor, eat the dinner that had been prepared for them—and not help clean up, then watch television for the rest of the evening.

Many a woman would also share that her husband always had high hopes for sex right about bedtime, but without any affection directed toward her all evening and no calls to check on her during the day. The wives complained, "My husband hardly notices that I'm in the same room with him until it's time to go to bed," confiding that their husbands would not show them any affection until they wanted sex.

Some women said they didn't even know what an orgasm was and that their husbands "couldn't last more than a few minutes, with hardly any foreplay." They commonly said that they only had sex to keep their husbands happy.

I had been lucky. I couldn't relate to these women. My husband was helpful, spent time helping the kids, and was great about everything that they said their husbands were not.

One warm, summer night, swinging with Greg on the front porch while watching the heat lightning, it dawned on me that one or more of my five daughters might find themselves in the same situation as my coworkers. Half-serious and half-joking, I challenged, "If any of our daughters end up with a husband that is unattentive, or if they don't give service to each other as they should, I'm going to sit down with them and make sure they know how to take care of each other's sexual needs properly!"

Greg threw back his head and laughed his great laugh. Knowing me well, he said, "That would be interesting. I'd like to be a fly on the wall to see that!" Never did he or I ever think that I would be in a position to actually do that.

By the time my daughters got married, I was comfortable with the subject matter. My unique perspective comes from combining my expertise in medical information regarding sexuality, my knowledge, my awareness of cultural and religious implications on sexuality, and my understanding of why successful sexuality is so important in marriage. It is interesting to realize that, years later, thousands of young couples have sought me out for precisely that information.

As young women seek guidance and information about the functioning of their bodies and sexual relations, I've also included their fiancés in the discussion portion of premarital appointments. This discussion is an excellent opportunity to start them on a good path to approachable and open discussions about sexual satisfaction in their marriage.

Sometimes, mothers of the bride-to-be would attend the premarital appointment. Often, they would tell me, "I wish someone had talked to my fiancé and me in this simple and clear manner before we got married. It would have saved us a lot of heartache and pain!" Though most were now satisfied with their sexual relationship with their spouse, some shared that the first months and years of their marriage had been frustrating—and sometimes even traumatic—because of pain from lack of arousal, a tight hymen, or the inability to orgasm.

More than one husband has confided in me that pleasuring his wife was his deepest desire. It was his expression of love to her. He was discouraged that he didn't seem able to meet his wife's sexual needs. It was frustrating for both of them. I also have had women of all ages, even in their sixties, share that they have never had an orgasm.

Before we get started on all the "good stuff" (Chapter Four: The Sexual Encounter), I want to suggest a healthy way to frame how you read this book and how you look at your own sexuality. Try not to apply preconceived ideas or experiences to what you read herein. Read with excitement and a thirst for knowledge. Read to understand as well as possible how to develop your sexuality and sexual relationship with each other.

Start by "owning" where you are currently, as you will be more open and teachable. If you have had previous sexual experiences, don't assume the relationship you are in or about to go into will be the same positive or negative experience as it was in the past. Open your mind and look forward to who is now in front of you. Read this book with a desire to learn and become the best lover that you can be.

Most people glean much of their information about sex from potentially unreliable sources. They learn by what their friends have told them; listening to other men or women talk; what their parents have taught them; watching television, movies, the internet; viewing or reading pornography; or from sex education at school. All of this can be skewed, depending on each person's individual experience. The reality is that sexuality within marriage is a new experience for both spouses—it is okay not to grasp what it will be like in every respect. Just know it will be an exciting adventure!

These reasons, plus being encouraged by my patients, other midwives, and physicians to write this book, have contributed to the "why" behind this book. The information contained in this book comes from the knowledge and expertise that I have gleaned from many years of listening to, observing, and caring for thousands of real, everyday women in everyday life. I have done this so that the content will be more personally relevant to you—the reader—and helpful, whether you are a man or a woman.

I do not believe that most healthy young men and women need extensive medical information about their sexual organs, diagrams of sexual positions, detailed descriptions on how to please each other, or a book about sexual problems and how to overcome them. Excitement and desire to enjoy your sexuality and please your spouse will carry you a long way down the road to "successful sex" (hence, the name of this book). You are intelligent, capable, and creative. With just a little guidance from this book, you will develop a great sexual relationship in your marriage.

2

THE SECRET TO GOOD SEX

Vulnerability, Trust, and Abandoning Oneself

Good sexual relations require *vulnerability, trust, and abandoning oneself to your sexual self.* The more vulnerable, honest, and open you are—and the more willing that you are to let go and abandon yourself freely—the more sexually satisfied that you both will be.

Letting go of inhibitions is paramount, and that means that the most private areas of your body, and private thoughts, are shared with your partner. Exploring them together will help you develop the most profound trust that you can create on this earth. Many refer to marriage as *two people becoming one flesh*. The things that you do with each other are sacred and are special for just the two of you.

Vulnerability and Trust

To illustrate these points, I'd first like to take a quick look at some non-sexual examples of vulnerability and trust. I will start with a simple case that doesn't have much consequence: Some women, before marriage, wouldn't dare let their future husband see how they look first thing in the morning—with no makeup, with crazy hair, and before brushing their teeth. Yet after a short time in marriage, they vulnerably share that part about themselves with him. Instead of the rejection or the displeasure that they once feared, they realize that their husbands love and accept them just as much, or more.

An even greater example of vulnerability might be sharing about a health issue. One of my patient's stories has always stood out to me.

During a premarital exam, I suspected an abnormality with Dyanne's reproductive organs. She had two cervical openings, which are usually associated with having an abnormal uterus. After ordering a CT scan, we found that she did indeed have two halves of a uterus, side by side, which is called uterine didelphys. It has serious implications for a high-risk pregnancy, where there is only a 60 percent chance of bringing home a live child with each pregnancy.

After reviewing her chart, I walked into the exam room with a heavy heart. I explained her results to her, including all the risks associated with her childbearing. She asked if she could bring in her fiancé so that I could explain it to him. I could almost see the vulnerability that she was feeling, thinking about how he might react when he found out that they might not be able to have the large family they wanted. We scheduled an appointment for them to come in together.

They arrived as scheduled. He was a muscular, 6'2" football player, appearing larger than life. I could sense the concern and love that he felt for his future wife. I explained the situation and the possible implications that it could have on their planned future family. I found myself preparing for the need to comfort her, depending on his reaction. After answering his questions, I asked him how he felt about all of it. He paused and looked at me incredulously with his strong features and said, "Do you think this would make a difference in my desire to marry her? Do you think I would love her any less?" He put his arm around her, and with emphasis, said, "I am marrying her. I am not marrying her uterus! I love *her*." And so, we come to a great litmus test for true love: "Do you love me even when I don't meet your original/natural expectations?"

I can still hear his words, making clear his acceptance and love for her. I can't think of a more vulnerable place for Dyanne to be. But instead of hedging or minimizing the seriousness of the situation, Dyanne was honest and vulnerable. Seeing the look of relief on her face that day was amazing: watching her vulnerability melt into complete adoration and trust. (As a wonderful conclusion, and though with some trouble with miscarriages at first, I was able to deliver five beautiful children for them.)

Sharing vulnerably with each other allows trust to develop. Whatever concern you have had in the past (or may have currently)—or if there is something that you are not proud of, where you feel guilt, shame, or fear—share it with your spouse. It will be liberating to you! It may be anything from stealing, to bad grades, to dishonesty, to a bad habit, to changed behaviors, to addictions, to family problems, to pornography use, to relationship problems, to a past belief system, or to fears or guilt about sexual behavior.

You might have apprehension and worry about the response that you may get when sharing. Instead of expecting the worst, think about how rewarding it will be to tell your fiancé or spouse something and have them respond with love, respect, and acceptance. That level of joy and intimacy is transforming!

Occasionally, the response is not a positive one. If this happens, understand that learning to trust and be vulnerable can sometimes take time, maybe even years. These challenges can strengthen your relationship with each other. Don't give up when you truly love each other, even though one or both of you may be struggling with an aspect. Get professional help if needed. And remember, honest vulnerability needs to be present to develop trust.

If there are situations where a negative response could be revealing an unreasonable or unhealthy person, sometimes the relationship will end, even with the commitment of an engagement having been in place. That is okay too, as constant red flags can alert you to long-term problems that are better off being resolved before marriage.

This same high level of vulnerability and trust is what propels sexual satisfaction in your relationship— your spouse needs to know all about your body and your needs without embarrassment or shame. Letting go and completely trusting your spouse is paramount.

Abandoning Oneself

Once you have developed trust in each other and allow yourself to be vulnerable, you can transition to *abandoning oneself to your sexual self.* Many people think of the term *abandon* as being forsaken or forgotten. However, to clarify in this text, it is reframed to mean *to abandon your self-conditioned boundaries.*

When you abandon oneself, you don't control the situation, and you completely let go of all of your inhibitions. It is especially important for a woman to understand the implications and effects of abandoning herself as it relates to her sexual experience, specifically orgasm. She must abandon her *control self* to her *sexual body self* and trust and believe that her body knows what to do naturally—and to not fight its responses. This act of abandoning must also be cherished by one another, in whatever form it takes.

If a woman is fearful that she might not move or act the way she is "supposed to" (whatever that is), the fear may interfere with her arousal state and her ability to enjoy the sexual encounter and orgasm. This concern and anxiety won't allow her to "let go." By being vulnerable to and developing trust in her husband, she can feel safe enough to abandon herself to her sexual body's needs.

It is important that she not be afraid to let her husband see all of her and realize the pleasure of knowing how much he loves who she is. She needs to be excited to allow her body to either move actively, or not as actively, or to move in ways that she hasn't moved before. She needs to know that it is okay if she makes noise during the sexual encounter or is quiet during sex. How her body responds will be unique to her (as will be his response to the sexual encounter). She must trust that her body knows what to do, allowing orgasm to overcome her and letting herself enjoyably yield, or *abandon herself,* to her own sexual power.

When a woman places pressure on herself to perform, she may not be able to surrender to this process. One suggestion to help her relieve her anxiety is to turn her focus to him initially. Centering her thoughts on him and his body can help her forget herself. The emphasis on his genitals and how she can stimulate him can lead to her own arousal.

However, eventually, she may need to concentrate on her own body and sexual thoughts. As her desire to orgasm increases, she must let her sexual body take over. Allowing herself to enjoy how he is pleasuring her (which he will love to do) and intensely focusing on how good and full her genitals feel helps her let go completely and orgasm. *Abandoning oneself* will result in a beautiful sexual encounter for both of them.

The key points are these:

- *Vulnerability*—have a desire to open your heart, mind, and body to your lover, and let go of any pretense regarding the sexual encounter.

- *Trust*—don't orchestrate or control the sexual encounter; let it be whatever it is going to be.
- *Abandoning oneself to the sexual body's self*—allow the sexual experience to take you over.

In summary, being *vulnerable, trusting,* and *abandoning oneself* must be rooted in all aspects of the relationship, then cumulates in the sexual encounter as an essential and necessary part of a marriage. This process of allowing vulnerability and openness, then receiving acceptance and love from the other partner, develops a trust that is beyond powerful.

3

REPRODUCTIVE PHYSIOLOGY AND ANATOMY

Each person has been given all that we need for our lives here on earth. Every part of our body was designed for a reason.

Some men and women have fears or concerns about the upcoming sexual encounter. A man might worry about satisfying his wife, not lasting long enough, or be afraid he might hurt her. A woman might wonder if it matters if she has an orgasm or if it is even "okay" to enjoy sex.

In this chapter, I will briefly present the importance of the sexual parts of the male and female body. In doing so, I hope that you can see that it was truly intended for both of you to not only orgasm but also to have a vigorous, healthy sexual relationship in your marriage.

We are all built basically the same; but, like the differences in our arms, legs, and face, we all have individual variations in our genitals. There is no correct look for your genitals. In most cases, both of you will appreciate each other just the way that you are.

I will briefly discuss the male reproductive anatomy, a bit more about the female reproductive system, and the primary key points that affect sexual relations. The diagrams below will be helpful for your reference.

The Male

Most male anatomy is easy to see and to observe how it all works. In general, men are easier to figure out and usually very easy to please sexually. It arouses a man to know that his wife is excited to participate fully in sexual relations with him. He wants to know that he pleases her and that she admires and needs him. Knowing that she loves the sexual encounter arouses a man the most and is very important to him.

Purpose of the Penis

Below is a basic drawing of the male genitalia (Figure 1). There are three main functions of the penis. They are:

- Being a passageway for urination,
- Producing sexual pleasure, and
- Delivering semen into the vagina.

When a man becomes sexually aroused, his brain sends nerve messages to stimulate the penis. On the bottom or underside of the penis, the two corpora cavernosa and the single corpus spongiosum (which houses the urethra) become engorged with blood. Along with this, some muscles surround the cavernosum and spongiosum to support the penis during erection. All of these actions together make the penis expand, harden, and assume an erect position.

The entire shaft of the penis is covered in nerve endings, but the glans (head of the penis) has more sexual nerve endings than anywhere else on his body. The super-thin layer of skin covering the shaft with all of these nerve endings is why men, at times, won't last as long into a sexual experience as women do. There is a specific area called the frenulum on the underside of the penis, approximately where the shaft meets the glans, that some men find especially sensitive. The glans is covered with a foreskin in an uncircumcised male, which "retracts" when an erection occurs. For a circumcised male, the foreskin has been removed, and the glans is constantly exposed.

The erection is necessary, or his penis would not be hard or stiff enough to deliver the semen inside of the vagina. After rubbing the penis for a period of time, he will climax with an orgasm. His orgasm results from the release of all the engorgement of blood built up inside the penis. Also, during orgasm, these same penis muscles contract to cause ejaculation, where the semen pushes out in pulsating waves far into her vagina. The semen will travel up through her cervix, into her uterus, and into the fallopian tubes in the effort to fertilize the woman's egg. The sperm can live anywhere from a couple of hours to as long as five days (in the right environment). After his orgasm is over, the penis relaxes over time.

After orgasm, most men are satisfied, want to relax or sleep, and it will be a while before they will be able to obtain another erection. However, some men only need a short time to obtain another erection.

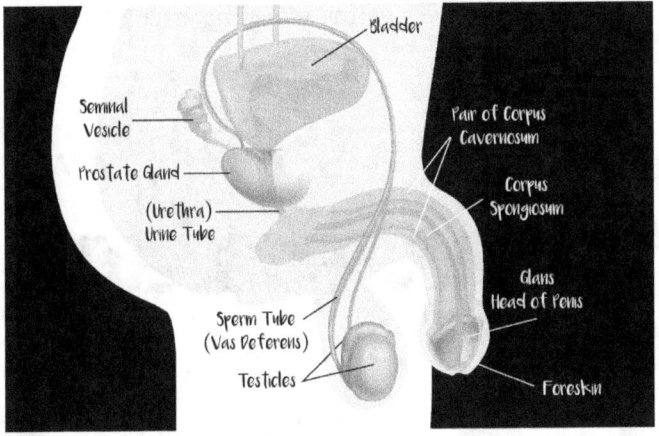

Figure 1—Male genital anatomy.

Purpose of the Testicles

The sperm originates in the testicles and passes through the vas deferens (sperm tube) to the penis. It picks up fluid and glucose along the way from the prostate gland and the seminal vesicle in order to form semen, which nourishes and facilitates movement of the sperm. Many sexual nerve endings surround the testicles.

Purpose of the Bladder and Urethra

Urine is collected in the bladder and passes through the urethra for urination. The urethra's use is for both urinating and delivering the semen by ejaculation.

The Female

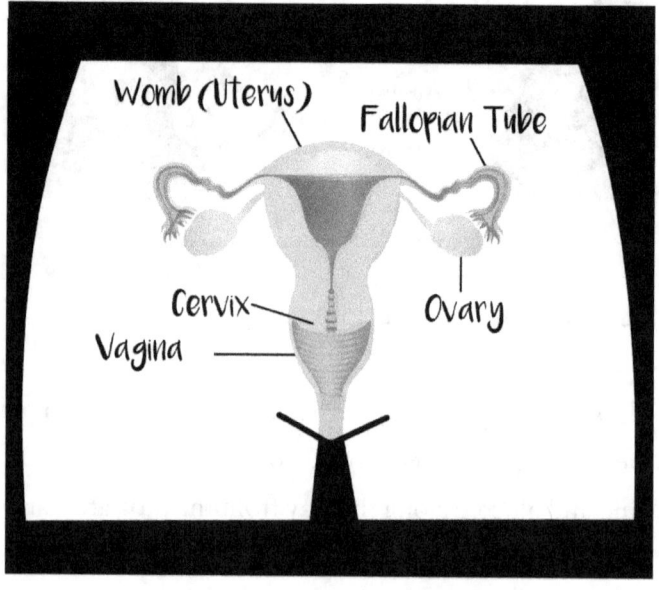

Figure 2—Female internal anatomy.

Purpose of the Uterus

The primary function of the uterus is for childbearing, as a womb to grow a baby. It is felt that the uterus contributes to the sexual experience from blood flow and release.

Purpose of the Cervix

The cervix holds the uterus closed but also opens to allow the baby through. Some women have increased sexual pleasure with stimulation to the cervix, which can occur with deep penetration of the penis during intercourse. However, other women find it uncomfortable or even painful if the cervix has too much pressure.

Purpose of the Ovaries

The ovaries are the center for most female hormonal regulation and release of the ovum (egg), about fourteen days before menses begins. A woman's unfertilized egg lives only twelve to twenty-four hours. For pregnancy to occur, either the sperm needs to be waiting for her to ovulate (the sperm hoping that he/she is the lucky one) or be there within twelve to twenty-four hours after ovulation.

These hormones that regulate the female cycle are powerful! Throughout the years, there have been many times that an unwed and pregnant teenage girl would relate that she had only had intercourse on one occasion. The question I received was always, "How could it have happened when I only had sex one time?" The ordinary person will doubt that pregnancy could occur this easily; but, believe it or not, it can.

One young woman, Suzanne, was nineteen years old. She arrived in the clinic alone, dressed casually but fashionably. I remember her wide, green eyes—clear and vulnerable. She told me that she had never been in a gynecological office before. This was her first sexual relationship. She sat in front of me with a puzzled expression on her face. "We only had sex one time! I don't know how we could possibly be pregnant." Her lips quivered with emotion. "We both wanted to wait to have actual intercourse until after we were married. We've passionately kissed, but we usually have had no problem stopping from going any further," she said, her eyes getting wet with tears. "I don't know what came over us. We both just started feeling like waiting didn't matter anymore." Shaking her head slowly, "I just couldn't think clearly and stop."

Suzanne's experience is the perfect example of the power and strength of hormones. Her hormones not only affected her, but they also affected Bill's response to her hormones. Let me further explain: During a woman's time of ovulation, there is a sharp rise—a one-day release of testosterone. This rise in testosterone increases her desire for kissing and sexual relations. It also causes her to create a pheromone (a mostly odorless, sexually stimulating smell), which draws her partner in, increasing his desire to have sexual relations with her. This process can also cause a decrease in the judgment processes during ovulation.

Purpose of the Breasts

Though the breasts are not part of the genitalia nor part of the internal reproductive organs, they are an important part of the sexual encounter both for women and men. A woman's breasts are not only used for feeding a baby; they also double as a truly sexual organ. They are sexually arousing to men, and most women (and some men) find an increase in sexual pleasure when the breasts are stimulated. Stimulation of the nipples assists with achieving orgasm by activating sexual sensory activities in the brain. Some women can even achieve orgasm this way.

The breast consists of lobules and ducts spread throughout fibrous and adipose tissue, along with special nerve endings in the nipple and areola (darker pigmented area). It is common for a woman's breasts to vary in size or shape or for one to be higher or lower than the other. Some women are concerned about what her husband will think if her breasts are different. Men don't care. In fact, they may appreciate that there is a choice of two different sizes.

Purpose of the Fallopian Tubes

The fallopian tubes sweep up the ovum (egg) released from the ovary(ies) and transport the egg to the uterus. Conception occurs between the sperm and egg while moving through the fallopian tube.

Purpose of the Hymen

The hymen (see Figure 3) is usually a thin, stretchable tissue that crosses the lower part of the vagina with a varied-sized hole in the middle of it. Usually, the opening is about the size of a small finger or a slender tampon. Some virginal women either can't insert a tampon into their vagina or find it painful on the first few attempts until the hole in the hymen has been stretched open enough to slide the tampon through. Though it can be uncomfortable for some, the hymen usually stretches open fairly easily during first intercourse. It also can tear, but it heals quickly, with only hymenal fragments remaining (Figure 4). For a few, the hymen can be thicker and cause problems when first married.

Patients have asked me many times, "What is my hymen for?" There is no known medical reason, and some feel it is a remnant of tissue left over from the formation of the vagina during embryonic development. However, I believe nothing is by mistake or "leftover"; all things in our bodies have a purpose. One thought is that the hymen is there to alert a woman because of the vulnerable situation that a woman can find herself in, whether with wanted or unwanted sexual advances.

It may start to hurt at the first attempt of penetration (particularly if not aroused), at which time she has to think twice about whether or not she wants to continue with this significant act of intercourse. Briefly, I believe it is given to women as a *check moment*. The hymen, though stretchable and penetrable, may cause this minor but initial barrier when the penis is trying to enter her vagina.

The hymen is not easily identified and is sometimes difficult for a medical provider to see. Sometimes it is felt on a one- or two-finger pelvic exam. The drawing below (Figure 3) shows the hymen's typical appearance on a virginal woman.

A common myth is that a woman's virginity is determined by whether or not her hymen is "intact" (hasn't been stretched or torn). Some women's hymen, even though virginal, is torn or stretched by tampon use, exercise, the insertion of fingers, or she may have only been born with a small fragment of tissue. A woman doesn't have to have an "intact" hymen to be a virgin. Suggesting an exam to verify virginity may be inaccurate, unfair, or harmful.

Though not necessary for everyone, some women desire to stretch the hymenal ring before marriage (see "Vaginal Health" in chapter six). Stretching may give her and her fiancé reassurance that their first act of marriage will be without pain or trauma. It is an easy maneuver that the woman can perform by herself. Penetration by the penis during intercourse will not feel any different to him at all, as it is the actual vagina that surrounds and massages the penis during intercourse, not the thin hymenal ring.

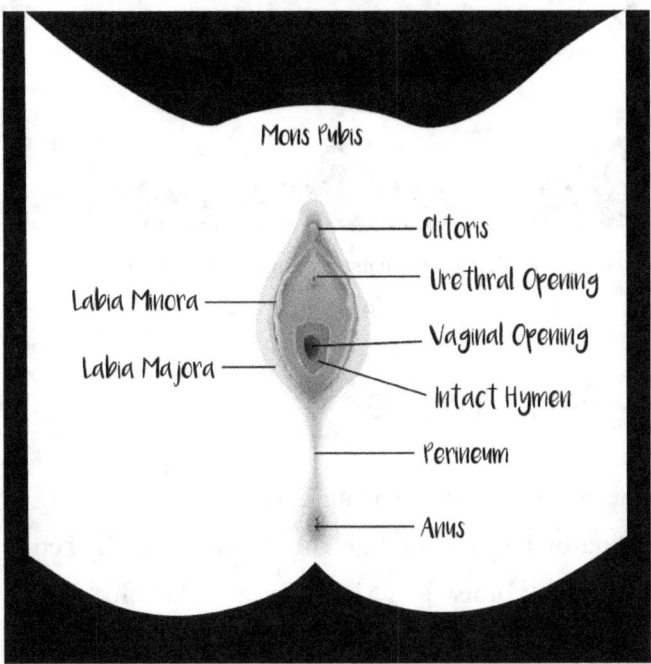

Figure 3—External female anatomy showing the hymenal ring still "intact."

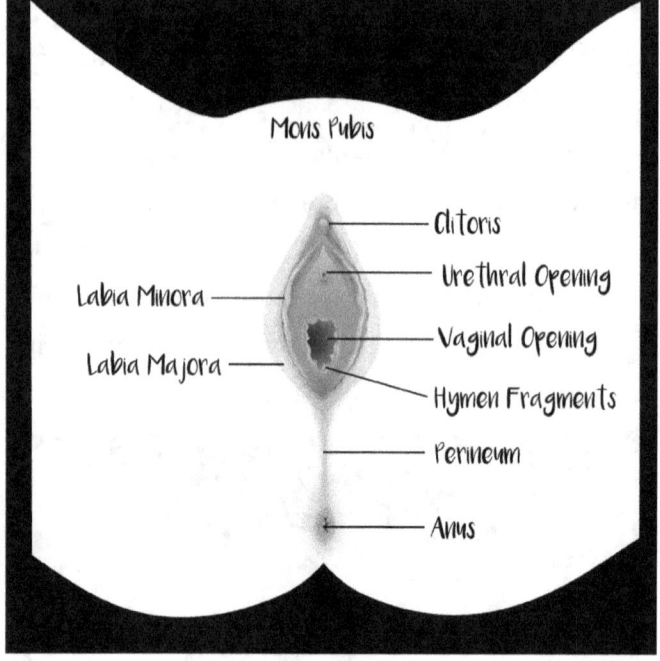

Figure 4—External female anatomy showing fragments of the hymen.

Purpose of the Vagina

The vagina is an amazing organ! When nothing is inside or passing through the vagina, its walls gently touch each other. It is a one-size-fits-all, from keeping the smallest tampon inside to allowing a baby to pass through. Afterward, it adjusts to just the size needed for satisfying a woman and her husband's needs during sexual relations.

Many men worry about if the size of their penis is the right fit within the vagina. They fear that they are too small to satisfy their wife or so big that they will hurt her. Out of all the thousands of women I have cared for, only a handful have shared that their husband's large penis caused discomfort. Most problems are resolved simply by making sure that she is aroused and ready before starting actual intercourse. Alternatively, I have never once had a woman complain about her husband being too small—never! As most of the female anatomy that responds to sexual stimulation occurs on the outside and in the lower part of the vagina, whatever size he is will be just right for her. Women are not worried about size; they just want a sensitive, attentive husband.

When aroused, the vagina will become very slippery and wet, opening and lengthening to receive his penis comfortably. Though he could, without causing her pain, enter her when this wetness is apparent, it is better to spend more time stimulating her until she truly wants him inside of her. Waiting for her to become lubricated naturally and fully aroused before starting intercourse also allows her to reach orgasm in less time. Some women, though aroused, will not lubricate easily, and may need help with additional lubrication (see "Vaginal Health" in chapter six).

Purpose of the Vulva

The vulva comprises the visible outer portion of the female genitalia. When using the term vulva, most generally refer to the *mons pubis, clitoris, and labia* (lips), as discussed below.

Purpose of the Clitoris

The clitoris is part of the vulva. The small tip of the clitoris (shown in the drawing), called the glans, is the only part of the clitoris that is seen and is comprised of more sexual nerve endings than found on any other part of her body. It has more nerve endings than on his entire penis. Many don't realize that there is more to the clitoris than what you can see—it branches downward, extends deep into her vulvar area, and all of it contributes to the sexual encounter and orgasm.

The clitoris is similar to his penis in its role in the sexual encounter and for orgasm. However, a woman's body is unique as the clitoris is designed for sexual stimulation only. The penis has three purposes—urination, reproduction, and sexual pleasure. A woman does not need the clitoris to urinate, have intercourse, conceive a baby, or give birth.

It becomes obvious that a woman was given a clitoris for only one purpose—for sexual pleasure! Why would she have a clitoris if she was not meant to enjoy its function? The clitoris is the only anatomical part of the human body that *its sole function is to provide sexual pleasure.*

Purpose of the Labia Minora and Labia Majora

The vulvar "lips" have an appearance that are visually sexually stimulating. Both the smaller inside lips and the fuller outside lips have many sexual nerve stimulators and contribute to sexual arousal when caressed. They also protect the soft and moist mucous membranes of the vagina. They become full and slightly reddened when aroused from increased blood flow to the area. This increased blood supply in the body can also cause a flush on a woman's upper torso, face, and neck when aroused (similar to how a man may flush when he is aroused).

Purpose of the Mons Pubis, Perineum, Buttocks, and Anus

The mons pubis, perineum, buttocks, and anus all have increased sexual nerve stimulators in general. When caressed, these areas may or may not have as intense a response as the vulvar lips but are pleasant and should not be forgotten in foreplay. She (or he, in applicable areas) may like stimulation in some of these areas.

4

THE SEXUAL ENCOUNTER

For the sake of impact, imagine that you are sitting in my office with your fiancé or spouse and that I am speaking directly to the two of you. I have personalized some of the following chapters by changing grammatical tense to help you *hear it* through that lens.

As we discuss the sexual encounter, you must understand that everyone is different. Each individual's achievement of a satisfying sexual experience is unique to them. So, please, no judgment on the right way to achieve climax or enjoy each other.

The Key Points

One of the essential parts of the premarital appointment is key but brief notes. If this is the only part of this book you read, you would most likely have enjoyable sex by following these simple but crucial guidelines.

Intimacy Helps

MEDICAL PRESCRIPTION FORM

Patient Name _____ Date _____

Address _____ Age _____

R𝗫

Intimacy Helps

Help her feel safe

20-40 minutes of foreplay

Talk to her

☺ Everytime!

Talk to each other

Careful of TV/phones, etc

Walk together

DISPENSE AS WRITTEN _____ MD

REFILL DIRECTIONS

DEA NO. _____

#1—Help Her Feel Safe

If falling into the virginal or newlywed category, your new wife may feel very insecure and vulnerable when arriving at where you will consummate your marriage. She has been taught to protect her body, which is in her instinct, even if she isn't aware of it. You must make her feel very safe so that her other instinct—to love and enjoy sexual relations—can come forward.

One of the ways to do this is to make sure that there won't be any interruptions. Make sure that your phones are off and not even in the room, where they may accidentally get connected to an unwanted phone call. Likely, she will want to know that the window blinds are closed and that the door to the outside is locked. If she is going to share herself with you freely, you do not want anything to inhibit this. She may want the lights low at first, even though you enjoy all the lights on! Reassure her that you will not do anything that would hurt and that you will take as much time as she needs and wants to be ready for you to enter her.

#2—Foreplay

For His Part of Foreplay

Twenty to forty minutes of foreplay before you enter her!

The above tip is not just for your honeymoon! Though not all women need this amount of time to be ready for penile entry or to orgasm, it is something that they may need to be a part of the sexual encounter whenever you make love. Typically, women take much longer than most men to become fully aroused. Occasionally, she will not need much time, but always be prepared to enjoy any amount of care needed for her.

Foreplay doesn't have to start in the bedroom. It can start whenever you show her affection and thoughtfulness, such as when you kiss, talk, touch, and make her feel beautiful. For those who are married, this can begin long before you actually go to the bedroom. If engaged, her body has probably been getting ready for intercourse each time you are near her, when kissing, or when your love for her makes her feel needed and wanted by you. After spending an evening together and saying goodnight, she may notice how slippery and wet her vaginal area is when using the bathroom before going to bed. When this wetness occurs, her vagina opens and lengthens in anticipation of you entering her. A response like this one is a healthy sign indicating that you are sexually compatible. She may not always get wet this easily, even when aroused (see "Vaginal Health" in chapter six); however, it is a reassuring sign that things will go well when the right time for sexual intercourse arrives for both of you.

The main focus of foreplay is to both emotionally and physically start connecting. Everyone is different in their preference; the main goal is giving attention to all of the areas that she feels are erogenous, by kissing or sensually touching them. These areas (depending on the person and her preference) can include her lips, eyelids, ears, neck, arms, breasts, stomach, genitals, inner thighs, buttocks, and more. Finding out which areas she enjoys the most is part of the fun! Taking time to caress and kiss all of the sensitive spots on her body will increase her desire for you to come back to attend to her genitals more. You could call this teasing, but keeping a variety in foreplay is always fun. Special attention to her genitals, especially her clitoris and learning what she likes, will be for only you to find out. Sometimes her clitoris can become desensitized by too much touching and rubbing. If this occurs, take a short break, turning your focus to other sexually sensitive parts. This allows the pleasurable response from clitoral stimulation to return.

Many women reach orgasm during foreplay, which is perfectly fine. Unlike men, who lose their erection after orgasm, she will still be aroused and ready for you to go inside of her, and she will still be very involved in the sexual encounter. Whatever she likes should be your goal.

For Her Part of Foreplay

You may have been taught to be modest, to hold your body sacred, and to avoid any sexual activity before marriage. If so, this may make you a little hesitant and shy at first, but don't be afraid to share your amazing female body with him. He is your husband, and this is something that only the two of you share. Open your legs and show him your entire body. Let him see how gorgeous you are! Women don't always feel that way about themselves—that they are gorgeous—but I guarantee that he will be fascinated by you and how you look. He will enjoy seeing all of you before, during, and after your sexual relations. He will think that you are the most beautiful woman on the earth! You should feel that way also.

I have observed men for forty-plus years watching their wives in labor when having a baby, which in itself is not a sexual event. However, I can see in their eyes how much they love their wives and how beautiful that they think they are, no matter what their shape or size. As a woman myself, I would not have believed how real this is if I hadn't observed it for all these years.

There is another aspect to seeing each other's bodies: Exploring allows a learning environment that encourages showing each other techniques that are personally satisfying. Let him know what feels good to you! As a woman, you must take charge of your own sexuality. Know that it is a good thing for you to love sex and to love your body. Enjoy getting to know how it responds to sexual stimuli.

It is just as vital that you spend time during foreplay attending to him. As typically the primary provider of foreplay, a man is genuinely happy to please his wife. Because of this, it is easy for a woman to forget to take time for him. Remember to make him feel beautiful too! He will adore any attention you can give to him. Men need two things: adoration and physical touch. Admire him! You can ask him what he likes, but most men are so happy to have you give his body any special attention at all. It would be rare for you to do something that he didn't like, barring a history of abuse (see "History of Sexual Abuse" in chapter five); so don't be afraid to look at him and touch him—spend time learning about what he likes. As he does for you, the main goal is for you to give attention to all of his erogenous areas by kissing or sensually touching them. Knowing that you are trying to please him makes him feel loved and is exciting to him.

Why So Different?

Along these lines, why is it that women generally take so much longer than men to become aroused or have an orgasm? Why were men and women designed so differently in this way? Why not make them similar so that their sexual needs and timings are the same? Wouldn't more similarity make marriage and life a lot easier?

I have pondered extensively on this. Nothing about your body is without a design and a purpose. You might consider these few ideas as the most likely answers.

Because many women take so long to become aroused or have an orgasm than their male partner, men may need to provide more effort and spend time just for her. Men learn that intimacy's goal is not to orgasm and finish but rather a time to be unselfish and serve their wives. A healthy, well-adjusted man is happy to provide sexual pleasure for his wife. It is a natural and fulfilling way for him to express outwardly his most sincere inward feelings of adoration and love for her. This is something that only he can do for her, and I guarantee you that it is gratifying for him! He absolutely enjoys it and looks forward to it. He knows that he is the only one that serves her in this way, pleases her, and shows her how much he loves her, which is very important to him.

On the woman's side, accepting this service from her husband causes her to feel a sweet indebtedness to him for the time and effort that he spends getting her aroused and bringing her to orgasm. Though some women are aroused and get wet very quickly, most take the twenty to forty minutes of foreplay discussed above. By taking this time for her, his actions make her realize just how much he truly does love her, and she feels grateful to him for his unselfishness and love.

This mutual give and take are an integral part of the sexual encounter every time, bonding a couple emotionally together. As his wife, she is amazed and cherished as the one receiving this love and act of service, and as her husband, he feels that her complete trust and abandoning herself to him is her reception of the love he is expressing to her. This is what brings joy to sexual satisfaction.

#3—Talk to Her, Help Her Focus

A man's voice is a turn on for a woman.

For centuries, women have swooned over male singers. From a man serenading his girl from below her bedroom window at her sorority house; to hearing a rough, sexy voice at a rock 'n' roll concert; to listening to a slow romantic ballad, women love a man's voice. Now you may not be a singer, but that doesn't matter to her at all. Just hearing your speaking voice when you are in conversation with her will warm her heart. I bet she prefers a phone call from you over a text every time! She will like hearing your voice, and she may especially enjoy it during your sexual encounter together.

A woman's thoughts are what excite her.

A person's genitals are stimulated by a soft caressing of the genital area, but the brain is where most sexual excitement occurs. A man can have an erection by random stimuli. Even something as simple as vibrations when riding a motorcycle or driving in a car can cause a spontaneous erection. Though not as common, a woman can find herself stimulated when sitting on a seat with movement or something similar.

However, to reach an orgasmic state, the genitals and other erogenous areas of the body need to communicate with the brain. Though valid for both of you, it is even more essential for women. Focusing with your mind on your genitals will help lead to a fulfilling completion of the sexual encounter.

Women can be thinking of a million thoughts during sexual relations. For example, she could be making her to-do list, worrying about a child's softball practice or piano lesson, what she will make for dinner, or even thinking about doing the laundry. She could also be worried about her body image and how you perceive her.

Though she may not be fully present, she may still be sexually stimulated enough to get wet and allow the penis to enter her without pain or discomfort. The movement of your penis inside of her will keep the vagina open and moist enough to continue intercourse. Still, she will not achieve orgasm if her brain isn't fully engaged in the process.

So, how to help her if this occurs? Talking to her during intercourse will keep her mind on the present and on you! Tell her how you have been looking forward to holding her and what you enjoy about her body. Remind her of how beautiful she is and how good her body feels to you. Share how sexual your own body and genitals are feeling during foreplay and while you are making love to her or any other thought that describes the current situation.

You could also describe sexual encounters that you have had together in the past that you particularly enjoyed or a fantasy about her and you. Encourage her to focus on the areas you are touching and visualize her vulva becoming aroused and full in anticipation of her release. All of these suggestions may make a significant difference in how quickly she becomes or stays aroused. If you talk to her during lovemaking, it keeps her attention on the sex that is going on in your bedroom and not about making the bed afterward.

Experiment with talking to her. Once she is more involved in the sexual encounter, you may focus on something else, but almost all women love hearing how beautiful and sexy they are! There are many times when you will be too passionate to talk, as you may want just to feel and enjoy all that is occurring.

#4—Every Time

"A good man takes care of his wife before he takes care of himself."

The above is an adage that I have used at every premarital appointment since I started practicing as a nurse midwife. It says it all, both in sex and in marriage.

Though a newlywed couple may try to orgasm simultaneously, this may have some drawbacks. A man may not be able to keep from having an orgasm right at first, as just the newness of her touching him can cause him to ejaculate early. He needs to learn soon how important it is that she has an orgasm before he does. Until he can learn control, I would encourage him to wait to orgasm until after she orgasms.

After orgasm, most men are satisfied and want to rest or sleep. Even if he tries, his decreasing interest becomes apparent to her. If she has not had an orgasm yet, it can be challenging for her to achieve an orgasm. This is true not only because of the penis becoming soft but because even when touching her, his passion for her lessens. This decrease in his drive makes her feel less attended to by him, possibly making her feel unfulfilled or dissatisfied.

So, please remember the saying above. Memorize it! If you feel that you cannot last very long with your penis rubbing inside of her, pull out and focus on bringing her to orgasm some other way before going inside of her vagina again. You can do this by touching, caressing, or kissing her genitals and other erogenous areas. That way, you can make sure she has been sexually satisfied before you ejaculate and lose some of your passion for sexual activity with her.

Another thought is to explore ways to stimulate her clitoris manually while you are thrusting inside her. Your wife may need this additional clitoral stimulation to bring her to orgasm during actual intercourse.

Suppose you do ejaculate before she has an orgasm. In that case, it is vital that you mentally and emotionally stay in the game! Sometimes she is right behind you in the timing of orgasm. If she isn't, take as much time as needed to bring her to orgasm manually. Never act like it is anything but fabulous to help her come to orgasm. She needs to know, without a doubt, how much you love doing this for her.

Another option is that, after a short period, you may be able to get an erection again, and your passion for her will return. Continue to caress and stimulate her until you can continue with intercourse. As I have repeated before, everyone is different, and your sexual encounter and orgasm may look a little different. Just remember, no matter *how*, you need to take care of her and make her smile—every time!

#5—Talk to Each Other

Intimately talking to each other is one of a woman's most basic needs and can open the door to her sexual desire. Though he becomes aroused with only a quick look, intimate conversation and affection are usually her stimuli.

Spending time in conversation is significant, not only during the sexual encounter but all of the time. Communicating with each other, both verbally and nonverbally, gives feedback about your preferences during your sexual encounters together. Talking to each other is crucial for keeping you moving forward toward continued better relations.

Tell each other when something is uncomfortable or painful, even when the same activity has been comfortable in the past. Pain is an arousal killer. It is essential that you let each other know how you feel—your spouse is not a mind reader.

Ask your spouse to show you what feels good so that you can learn what they like. Sometimes, during your sexual encounter, you will want soft touching and, other times, firmer pressure. If you aren't sure what type of touch arouses you, experiment together. Take turns stroking or kissing while sharing what you have discovered. Remember, whatever you do to explore yourself and each other when together is part of the sexual encounter. It is all about sharing. If you were to go off alone and have a sexual encounter by yourself, it leaves the other person out of the experience. I would encourage you to experiment together, to reap the closeness it can bring.

You are her man, and she is your woman. Learning your spouse's tastes and pleasures is for only you to know. On the other hand, though a lot will be the same, don't be surprised if next time one of you might like things a little different—that is why the sexual encounter can be so much fun throughout your lifetime!

Most couples try hard to please each other. Sometimes you may worry that you might hurt each other's feelings by sharing that you are uncomfortable, feel awkward, or don't like something. Agree to a rule that allows your spouse to give you directions, especially positive feedback, suggestions, and occasionally corrections. Always receive this sharing, coaching, and questioning with openness and love. In fact, encourage it! Remember, this emotional bonding is ultimately what sex is all about. Being a good listener and a safe recipient builds that connection even more.

Earlier I mentioned that a poor body image and repeated negative thoughts about your body could deter focusing and achieving orgasm. If this arises, the best antidote is an open conversation about it. Asking your spouse—and hearing the answer—will absolve negative thoughts, enhancing your pleasure together.

For example, she may be concerned that he finds her stomach unattractive, worrying about it during every sexual encounter. In reality, he probably hasn't even paid specific attention to it. If he has, he most likely enjoys how it feels and looks. She is his wife, and most men love everything about their wives' bodies.

There is a chance that your spouse may not have an entirely positive response that you feel is ideal for every concern you bring up. That is also okay! It opens up an opportunity for growth and discovery—to know each other more intimately. Suppose that you don't like something about them or a particular thing that they do. In that case, it is much better to talk about it openly than constantly worrying about it. Where is the reward in feeling loved by someone that, deep down, you feel like doesn't even know your true self or your true thoughts? Creating closeness and intimacy in a marriage comes from being willing to know your partner and be known. Talking to each other is a big priority!

#6—Beware of Televisions, Phones, and Electronics

One of the main issues that marriage therapists deal with is what many call a "time-starved" relationship, as discussed by Drs. Les and Leslie Parrott in their book *Your Time-Starved Marriage: How to Stay Connected at the Speed of Life* (Zondervan, 2015). If you find more often than not while in a room together that you are watching television while your spouse is playing on their phone or texting with friends, your marriage can slowly die from lack of nourishment. As the Drs. Parrott expressed in their book, couples that have distractions starve their relationship to death.

Also, as discussed before, thoughts in your brain are what the sexual encounter is all about. That is where the real excitement lies, and the brain orchestrates all of it. If you take away thoughts of each other when you are together, such as being distracted by your phone or watching television, it can interfere with your desire to have sexual relations. Get in the habit of putting your phones/screens away when you are together—including at mealtimes. A "no-screen bedroom" can create a shelter away from the world. Talking, laughing, loving, and lovemaking will all happen more readily if you don't retreat to screens. Remember, intimate affection and conversation are usually two of her most basic desires that, once met, help open the door to her sexual self.

For example—Chad and Natalie spend the evening watching a scary movie in their bedroom before going to sleep. Natalie gets up to finish getting ready for bed, and her thoughts are on what she was watching on the television. She isn't thinking about him or sex at all. Chad sees her getting undressed and is immediately aroused, and wants to have sexual relations with her. When Natalie returns to bed, he approaches her intimately. She can't believe that he can think of sex when she is still upset from the scary show they just finished watching together!

Now remembering that it takes most women at least twenty minutes to go from not having any thoughts of sex to being aroused enough for intercourse, it will take some time and some intensive action on his part to get things going. She also needs to switch her mind off her other thoughts. Even at this point, she may not be willing, depending on the amount (or lack thereof) of cuddling and interaction between them prior to and during the movie.

Instead, they would have more likely moved to a sexual encounter if they had spent some time in conversation along with physical contact with each other. This concept is also true during a meal, when a conversation can flow easily if no electronics are present. If he has been attentive to her, she may be the one to initiate sex, wanting to connect with him physically and sexually, as her conversation needs would be met, which opens the door to her sexual desires. An example of this leads me to the last note on the list.

#7—Walk Together

"Couples that walk together stay married longer."

I don't know where I picked this tidbit of truth from, but doing this will significantly improve a couple's relationship satisfaction. This saying represents not only the implications of walking together but also relates to the quality and amount of time you spend with each other.

For example, I ask my young couples in my clinic, "A woman has been home all day with two children, and her husband comes home from work and offers to go for a walk. Why will their marriage improve?" Their responses vary, from "the couple talking with each other," to "holding hands while walking," to "spending time having fun recreating together," to "getting outside in the sun with the benefits of exercise." These are all valid, but another result that these young couples do not think of is what happens later.

When arriving back home after spending time with him, most women have an increased desire to be close to their husband. Spending quality time with him increases her "like" for him and creates an emotional connection between them. It also is the way she stimulates her sexuality. She thinks to herself, "He is so wonderful! He came home after a long day, pushed the stroller for me, talked with me, and made me feel cared for and valued. He is so kind, and I love him so much. *Let's go make love!*" Believe it or not, that is how it works.

Every time that I have shared that example with

a longtime married woman, such as the bride's mother, she laughs outright, agreeing with the underlying thought. Chatting with thousands of women about this, I have heard a common theme: What turns a woman on is thinking about how much she loves her husband, the time he spends with her, and all that he does for her and their family. While thinking about having sex also arouses her, walking together, talking to each other, and sharing time together creates the emotional bond that gives her the *desire* for sexual relations. Women have the passion and desire for sex just as much as men. They just approach it differently. If a man could never forget that quality one-on-one time spent with his wife—making that connection—is what makes her want to have sex with him, they will both be more happy in the long run.

"I tell couples that if, from the beginning of their marriage, they would walk together and have dinner together every night, they would likely never need me."

— Matt Eschler, LMFT

Orgasm—A Climax of Sexual Excitement

It is incredible how so many nerves conduct information from the genitals to the spinal cord, to the brain, and then back and forth for an orgasm to occur. Even the most complex invention made by man pales compared to the intricacies of the human sexual encounter, starting with the arousal state through to the culmination of orgasm.

It is generally considered that women have two types of genital orgasms: clitoral and pelvic floor orgasms. Still, many details have evaded researchers for a century. Trying to correctly determine what occurs in each woman during her highly complex and personal sexual experience is impossible for anyone to define.

I cannot stress enough the importance of realizing that one type of orgasm may feel better to her than the other. Women enjoy a variety of sensations. Though the vast majority of women have orgasms arising from their clitoris, others will have more of a vulvar-perineal-vaginal-cervical (general pelvic floor) orgasm. Remember that the clitoris branches down through the vulvar area, resulting in sexual sensations throughout her entire genital area when stimulated. There are also times when women occasionally enjoy the intimacy of the sexual encounter without choosing to have any type of orgasm.

While the penis is thrusting inside her, there is a pulling and rubbing of all the outer and inner parts of the female genitalia. This movement and rubbing will cause some women to orgasm with intercourse alone. However, many women desire additional stimulation of the clitoris in some manner, either with or without him being inside of her, to achieve orgasm.

Most of the vagina's nerve endings are in the lower third of the vagina, including the G-spot (Grafenberg spot). Though the vagina is not like the outer part of a woman's genitalia (the vulva), which is saturated with sexual nerve stimulators, it can still contribute to the sexual experience.

There is a lot of hype about the G-spot and the blended orgasm. I am addressing it here because, though the clitoris is known and preferred by most women as the most significant contributor to orgasm, the G-spot is an actual spot that many couples have searched for to no avail. The vagueness of the G-spot does not mean she is not enjoying its benefits; she just may not realize that she is.

This spot is located on the anterior/top/upper part of the vagina, about an inch inward from the outside opening of the vulvar lips. It feels like a soft, smooth small bean-sized tissue when she is not aroused. It can bother some women to have it touched too much, as it may make her initially feel like she needs to urinate. After stimulating by applying firm, rhythmic pressure or stroking with fingers (or this may naturally occur with the thrusting of the penis), that feeling can eventually go away. This spot turns into a firmer area, which, when released, contributes to the pelvic floor climax.

Throughout the years in my gynecological clinic, women randomly ask about this during their office visits. Many have reported similar-sounding sensations contributing to their overall sexual experience during intercourse. Still, many women question whether or not they know the location for sure, as they may not have found an actual "spot" as described above. They all report noticing and enjoying different sexual sensations when using varying positions and with stroking and pressure applied in that area. If tension builds and a release does occur, she will experience some type of orgasm. However, as stated above, almost all women express that the clitoral glans is the most significant and preferred contributor to their sexual experience.

When women have regular orgasms and love their sex life, they don't worry about achieving a specific type of orgasm. Their focus is on having a fun, meaningful experience, which will result in her enjoying whatever kind of orgasm occurs. Doing this avoids overanalyzing the sexual encounter, which, in turn, detracts from the overall experience.

Every time that you make love together, the response in your body varies, and the sexual encounter feels new and exciting. What happens one time may not occur the same way the next time. It can be nice to have different experiences while arousing and satisfying each other in this very intimate way.

Multiple Orgasms

A male friend of mine once said that you only want more than one orgasm before having an orgasm. However, he is a man speaking. After a man ejaculates, he needs a period of rest before he can become erect again. Sometimes, just a few minutes pass; but, typically, it can be much longer.

A woman can be satisfied with one orgasm, but there are also other times when a woman wants multiple orgasms during one sexual encounter. She should honor her sexual inclination, whether she feels satisfied after one orgasm or if she desires more.

It is easy to physically see when a man is sexually satisfied, as his penis becomes soft. In women, it is harder to tell physically. The vulva may become swollen from the normal engorgement that occurs during arousal. This engorgement is not apparent in all women. One way to learn is for her (or her husband) to feel her genitals and compare how her vulva and perineum feel when she is aroused versus when she is not aroused. It is easier to observe in women who have previously been pregnant. However, the best way to know if she needs another orgasm is if she *wants* more!

Though I always encourage men to help their wife have an orgasm with every sexual encounter, there may be times that she may want a pass. She may just simply want him inside of her, feeling the closeness that comes with just holding each other. There is no right way! No one else is her—*let her decide*. Due to his strong desire to please her, he wants to show his love by helping her achieve orgasm. He should refrain from managing her sexuality—it is hers that she shares with him.

It doesn't matter what type or how many orgasms she has. Once the sexual tension is released completely, neither of you will find that you need another orgasm . . . until the next time.

Avoiding Goal-Oriented Sex

I would like to address some sexual intentions that, though credible, may hinder the real and present sexual experience by focusing on "the goal" too much. I will list a few below:

- Simultaneous orgasm—though this is fun to do, alternatively, you may find that you concentrate even better on your partner when you are not having an orgasm at the same time. Also, she may feel the need to have more orgasms. At that point, if he has already ejaculated, it might be hard for him to continue his passion for her and bring her to orgasm *(as discussed earlier in Key Point #4).*

- Multiple orgasms—though she may have multiple orgasms, she may be satisfied with one. As I noted earlier, let her decide!

- G-spot orgasm—just the experience of trying to figure this out can be stimulating to both of you. Still, you are not alone if you never figure out exactly where her G-spot is. Some women, frankly, don't prefer it.

- The blended orgasm—this is where a woman has both a clitoral and G-spot orgasm simultaneously. As discussed, this may happen naturally during intercourse. It depends on where the penis is rubbing in her vagina and whether or not his body is stimulating her clitoris simultaneously. It can also occur by manually stimulating both the clitoris and inside the vagina simultaneously. Not many women report knowing for sure whether they have experienced this, and they don't seem to care, as long as they are sexually satisfied.

- Having a preconceived way of looking, acting, or responding during your sexual encounter.

Let your sexual encounter occur uniquely as a

couple. Don't get hung up on the stigma of doing it right or doing it better. Just remember, it is all good if you both enjoy, feel happy, and are satisfied with your encounter.

The Importance of Liking Sex in Marriage

"A man needs to have sex to feel loved, and a woman needs to feel loved to want to have sex."

I don't know the author of this maxim, but it is another one of the simple pearls that I hope that you both remember for the rest of your life. However, don't misinterpret it. There is a common stereotype that a man's biggest priority is sex and that women don't have as much need for sex as men. *That stereotype is not accurate*. In the saying above, they *both need and want sex*. It is the understanding of how each of them arrives at the point of sexual desire and clarifies how they obtain the feeling of love for one another that is the secret!

For example, women will talk and giggle about what their husbands think would be the best Valentine's Day gift that he could give her—great sex; because, to him, that is the ultimate gift! He may take her to dinner and buy her a gift, but still, to him, the ultimate gift is making love to her. She will also love the sexual encounter, but she also enjoys the leading up to it—it is necessary to her. It is what makes her want to have a sexual encounter with him.

In the over-forty years that I have practiced, I have met only three men that did not seem to care about how sexually satisfied their wives were. Their wives loving sex with them is what most men want more than anything! Because of how much *men need sex to feel loved*, he feels that the ultimate gift is spending time bringing her to orgasm—that is how he shows her just how very much he loves her. It truly is his physical way of showing his ultimate adoration for her.

If she doesn't enjoy the sexual encounter, he may continue with intercourse because of his need to ejaculate. When this happens, the act can feel empty when she is present in body but not in her heart. In this case, her own sexual needs aren't met, and he may believe that he is incapable of satisfying her. This can cause him to feel unfulfilled. He can become very frustrated and often doesn't know what to do. Most men are willing to try anything to help their wife have an orgasm—to have her be sexually satisfied; because that is *how he feels loved—by having sex.*

However, women may value other aspects of their sexual relationship regarding what *makes her feel loved.* For her, having him show affection, kindness, and engagement *is what excites her.* Intimate affection together with confidential conversation, such as going to dinner, holding hands, and kissing while you walk, is what she may need to increase her *desire to have sex.*

When this doesn't occur, she may feel anger or resent that he doesn't spend quality time with her before wanting or initiating sexual advances. She may not feel valued, except for when he wants sex.

For women and men, getting in the habit of being present only in body but not fully participating in either the sexual encounter or in meaningful conversation and connection can slowly break down your relationship with each other. This can occur through interruptions by children or the phone ringing, insufficient time, or hormonal changes, amongst other reasons. These interruptions are not the end of the world - they happen. Still, you both must make all the efforts that you can to be present continually and engaged in both mind and body before, during, and after the sexual encounter.

As Willard F. Harley, Jr. discusses in his book *His Needs Her Needs, Building an Affair-Proof Marriage*, three things can happen if a couple doesn't meet each other's needs, such as when she won't have sex often enough for him, or if he doesn't spend enough time snuggling and holding her. He suggests that there are only three choices for either of them:

1. They live unfulfilled, without their needs being met.
2. They find other places to obtain what they need.
3. They divorce each other.

None of these options are acceptable! Though these three choices present in a slightly fear-based manner, I feel that they are worth mentioning, as they can be a good wake-up call. Realizing each other's priorities and trying hard to meet those priorities is a continual goal for everyone who is married.

One thing to remember about this: Neither spouse should be having sex out of fear of losing their spouse to someone else, and sex should never be a "duty" or done out of fear. Instead, learn to care for and love one another. Recognize that sex, cuddling, talking, having fun together, or anything important to your spouse should motivate you to try harder out of love and concern for each other. Willingly serving each other will build connection, love, and appreciation for one another.

Another aspect to remember is that one spouse most likely will want sex more than the other in your relationship. *Expect it and accept it.* This difference is normal, and it may alternate and change throughout your life, depending on stressors and environment, along with how you treat each other. No matter what you do, this may always present itself as unbalanced to your relationship. Recognize and understand it while working with each other.

Be aware that the desire for sexual relations can be affected by:

- Hormone levels, which vary not only per individual but also on different days of the month, as well as during pregnancy, while breastfeeding, and when in menopause.
- Stressors in life.

- Not spending enough one-on-one time with one another.
- A lack of exercise.
- An unhealthy diet.
- Body image. (Remember, our bodies can change over time, and, though different than when we were younger or after having a baby, they are not better or worse. Allow yourself to enjoy these changes, to have even more wonderful sexual experiences as time goes on, as you learn more about each other.)

There are some things that you can do to increase your desire to have sexual relations with each other. All the things that I have discussed in the book about attentiveness to each other significantly contribute to increased desire. I will also be discussing a few more ideas later. However, there is one thing specific to sexual desire that you can do throughout your whole marriage that can be very helpful.

*"The more you think about sex, the more
you want sex.
The more you have sex, the more you think
about sex."*

Believe it or not, the above hypothesis is true! The gem to learn here is that, if you are the one with less desire for sexual relations, train your brain to think about sex more often. Even put it in your calendar, where you pause throughout the day to dwell on your last sexual encounter together. This thought can't be a rushed "to-do" item. Even a minute or two thinking about your favorite time together sexually, how you felt when you were building your relationship, or fantasizing about having sexual relations in the future, can significantly increase your sexual thoughts. Calling each other and briefly sharing how much you enjoyed sex the night before, with details, etc., helps keep things alive and moving. Whatever people spend their time thinking about gets bigger. Encouraging these thoughts will lead to more sexual encounters together, which in turn will lead you to more sexual thoughts about each other.

5

KEEPING IT REAL

The "Experienced" Partner

When one or both of you have had a previous sexual experience, it is not uncommon for you to have concerns about your honeymoon. Just because someone has had sexual relations before doesn't mean that they know how to have, or how to help their partner have, a satisfying sexual experience. Having previous sexual experiences can sometimes keep a person from being open to learning more or lead them to having unrealistic expectations. They may also feel remorse, guilt, or shame about past experiences. Left unspoken or unaddressed, this potential may hinder the new relationship.

Many have insecurities about their fiancé's or spouse's previous partner. There is always the question of "How do I compare?" There are also the questions of "Will I be as good of a sexual partner as they had before?" and "Will he/she love me as much as he/she loved them?"

I was twenty years old when I married my late husband, Greg, who was twenty-five years old at the time. He had been previously married at nineteen and then divorced at twenty. He had shared with me that his ex-wife had started going out with friends and then eventually a male friend. When Greg found out about the male friend, he left his ring on the table and left. He did not try to work it out.

Greg told me that he had not been an attentive husband but rather came home from work, would read a book, and didn't have a lot of conversation with her. In retrospect, he understood why she had found another way to meet her needs. He was determined not to let that happen in our marriage.

When I first married Greg, I couldn't believe how close our feelings were. Never before had I experienced such strong, intimate feelings. The awe of the power of those feelings—they were so fantastic and real.

Then the thought came to me, "He was married to her before he was married to me. He must have felt this same passion and desire for her, just like I do for him now." A seed of jealousy started to take a small hold within my heart and began to create doubts.

I decided to approach the subject with him. I asked him if he had ever felt about her the way he felt about me. I was not sure if I wanted to hear the answer, as it wouldn't be the right answer no matter what he said. I will forever be grateful to him for what he taught me at this moment.

After thinking and considering my question for a long time, he said in the kindest voice, "Laurie, what is the purpose of this question?"

I instantly realized that I was being prideful—comparing myself and our new relationship to his ex-wife and his relationship at nineteen years old. I still wanted to hear that I was "better" and that he loved me more. Of course, he had felt love for her—he'd married her!

He then asked, "Where is this question going to take us? Is it down a good road or a bad road?"

As I pondered his question, I understood that he

was right: There was no point in having any discussion about this. No matter the answer, it would take us down the wrong path. I just had to be content with the present—with what was REAL and what was NOW.

Your previous relationships should have little or no bearing on what happens in your marriage. Only the current love and relationship you are in now should be the focus. Anything else only distracts you and takes you away from reality.

Consent and Being True to Your Moral Conscience

Deciding what you want to participate in and are comfortable with during your sexual relations has to be agreed upon between the two of you. The details of what you may or may not be comfortable with are beyond the scope of this book, but it's worth being aware that the differences are real and valid; a healthy relationship is one that honors them. A couple should not engage in sexual activity if either of these two reasons is present:

- You simply don't like or desire an activity, or
- It goes against your moral conscience.

In regard to the second reason, it would be devastating to a couple to have one person feel that they are doing something immoral or wrong, that goes against what they think is right for them and right with God.

I have observed what is considered moral or immoral within most religions regarding sexual encounter behaviors. Overall, the consensus requires that all of these be a reality:

- It involves only the two of you. (There is a popular theory that having more than two people in a sexual relationship will work if all partners agree. This is principally false. Polyamory, whether real and physical or mental and fantasized, typically doesn't work in the end.)

- You care more about your spouse's needs than your own.

- You individually identify your own "moral conscience" and what sexual activities you are comfortable with.

- Kindness and consideration for each other's feelings are of paramount concern.

- Both of you respect each other's boundaries.

- Asking yourself, "Are either of us compromised or demeaned because of my activities?"

- You never try to control your spouse.

Throughout this book, I have written reasons and ideas for why it is essential to try and please each other sexually. Because you love each other, you may go ahead with their request even when you don't desire the same thing at the moment. Your desire to please may cause you to be afraid to refuse a request from your spouse. The consequence is that, unintentionally, you do things against your moral conscience.

Doing something against your own will has the opposite effect on your relationship than what the sexual encounter was designed to do. Sex is about trying to bring you closer to each other. Engaging in unwanted behavior or actions that you are uncomfortable with will put a wall up between you—you won't feel safe. In a loving relationship, your spouse will never want you to go against your moral conscience. It is critical that you communicate effectively and honestly. Don't say what you think that they want to hear—tell the truth—it is always the best way.

As you learn more together about the sexual encounter and become more comfortable with each other, you can explore how you feel about different aspects of it. Know that it can be common to change how you think about your sexual activities over time. Searching your conscience will allow you to decide what works for you; and make sure that you discuss it with your spouse.

You can try to fulfill your spouse's desires and wants, but it is ultimately an individual choice. If you do not feel peace in your own mind, then resentment, guilt, and other negative thoughts and feelings about yourself or your spouse can interfere in your relationship. It is paramount that both of you are comfortable with whatever sexual activity you participate in.

Pornography

"Connection is the antidote—connection with each other, with God, and emotionally with yourself."

— Shauna Watson, pornography life coach

In the reality of today's world, young couples need to recognize that pornography is everywhere. It distracts from what is real in front of you, deceiving you into seeking worth and comfort in the wrong place.

Pornography brings someone else into what is meant for one man and one woman.

My goal in including this section in this book is to shed some light on the subject. I hope that it will open the door to dialogue with each other and encourage you to get help as needed.

Most people who view pornography are not addicted to it but are caught in a trap, using it as a buffer against stressors in life. Some hope that once married, any concerns or compulsion about pornography use will resolve. This is a myth. You must discuss together whether either or both of you are currently seeking out or have previously viewed pornography.

Talking about this can be an incredible opportunity to create a genuine connection with each other. You will feel extremely vulnerable when you first open up to each other about it, but that is the first step to developing trust with one another.

Be genuine and honest, not shameful. In some cultures, the guilt is worse, as you feel you are a terrible person or aren't "enough." However, belittling how you think about yourself will not help, as it adds to the problem because of the shame associated with it.

If you feel shame, it can perpetuate the continued

participation in porn. The *pattern of losing oneself* in porn may help you escape and feel good momentarily, but the shame and negative emotions return magnified. This repeated pattern of shame fleetingly resolves by using porn again . . . and the cycle continues. *Diffusing the forbidden, the shame, and the isolation* are what help a person move beyond. Discussing your urges to use pornography with your spouse clearly reduces the power that porn has on you and your relationship.

Though there are some valid concerns, don't panic if you just discovered your fiancé's or spouse's current or history of pornography use. As someone who is not a user of porn, yet is committed to someone who is or has been, you may feel that this is an end-of-the-world scenario and that your relationship is doomed. Just remember that no matter how devastating it sounds, people and couples can heal from this. With some earnest efforts on both sides, you can work it out together. Though it can be big, try not to make it bigger than it is. The fact that someone feels safe enough to talk about it and trust you is an essential first step.

In cases like these, there are some critical points that the non-porn-participating spouse must realize. One is that your partner seeking out porn has nothing to do with you, your body, or your behavior. The other is that you need to have compassion and love for yourself by recognizing and validating how hard this can be for you and then obtaining outside support and counseling as needed. You must remember to take care of yourself as a non-participating partner. Honor and address any feelings that you have.

There are primarily two scenarios of pornography use that couples encounter, which will need to be addressed accordingly; speaking to the individual who has used porn:

- You may have viewed pornography but no longer have a need to pursue it. It may be something that presents itself periodically, but you do not seek it out. If relations with your spouse are open, you will feel safe to tell them if you start to feel urges to view porn or if porn periodically presents itself. This transparency will help diffuse the compulsion to use it. Be alert about where you are and how you are doing personally, and remember: the power of pornography will diminish when brought into the light.

- You may actively engage with porn and *are currently seeking it out either periodically or compulsively*. You know how to find the type of porn that interests you. Both periodic and compulsive levels of engagement with porn need active management, but the compulsive user may need more intervention. Be realistic about your situation to know where to start the healing process. Know that resources and help are available, such as podcasts, life coaches, groups, books, counseling, clergy, and other assistance. Start this process before marriage if possible. Most important for you to remember: There are people who have worked past this addiction—you are of worth; you matter; you are a loved son or daughter of God. Feeling bad and shameful beyond the remorse that helps incur a healthy change will not help you! Regardless of whether you fit in any of these areas, healing can happen.

Speaking now to the individual who is not a porn user: Be a safe person for your fiancé or spouse. Suppose that you are defensive or react with blame or condemnation. In that case, it will not go well, and there will not be any more vulnerability, trust, and connection developing between you. Avoid even the temptation to joke about it, as doing so can cause the other person's trust to erode.

Listen and be present and available for them. Avoid shaming comments, saying instead phrases such as, "Thanks for sharing," "Help me understand your feelings," "I'm glad that you told me," or something similarly safe.

Also, loneliness and boredom are setups for viewing porn. Think of the woman who catches her husband viewing porn and sends him to sleep on the couch—she doesn't need to make love with him, but maybe question the couch punishment. If neither partner is lonely, and both work on never being bored in an unhealthy way, you can eradicate porn from addiction levels.

Because pornography gives an unrealistic, skewed perception about the sexual encounter, avoid asking your spouse to participate in something you saw acted out in a porn scene where your spouse might be uncomfortable. Many women in my clinic have expressed that they feel judged and compared to the women viewed on the screen. Worse, they feel alone and abandoned when their husband participates in pornography. As a women's provider, I have more frequently heard the women's perspective of being the partner of a porn user. Still, it is becoming increasingly common for women to be engaged in pornography use. They can have just as many challenges associated with it.

There is some thought (hypothesis-media-based encouragement) that a couple can use pornography to help increase sexual arousal in each other. However, over time, more and more explicit material is needed to arouse each other. This can decrease a couple's ability to reach an arousal state independent of pornography.

Along this same line, a woman shared in my clinic that she and her husband would read sexual stories together (soft porn) to arouse themselves and get them in the mood for sex. She shared that though it would excite and arouse them faster, she did not feel focused on him due to being distracted by the thoughts of the story. Sharing her sexual experience with the story's characters robbed their relationship of intimacy with each other. She found more connection with her spouse when not using the stories. In line with my recommendations in this book, there are much healthier, more meaningful ways to develop intimacy, arousal, and sexual enjoyment.

I again want to emphasize the importance of

openness and honesty to avoid disconnection from your spouse. Make sure you take an active role in addressing any ongoing pornography use. Light always overcomes darkness! You can either have a relationship with porn or a real relationship with your spouse. Choose what is real—each other! If you are reading and discussing this together, you are already taking the first step. Congratulations!

History of Sexual Abuse

Sexual abuse can affect all ages and genders. Most abused persons will not come to the marriage with Post Traumatic Stress Disorder (PTSD), but most relationships will have to be tender and watchful as they progress down the paths of sexual intimacy. A history of abuse that is sexual or violent, especially from an intimate partner or a person that should have been safe and protective, can lead to trauma responses during sexual encounters. For example, a person who is forced to perform a particular sex act may react with fear, disgust, shutting down sexually, or even behave provocatively in response to an intimate moment. These trauma responses to beautiful moments can devastate a new spouse who now feels responsible for the pain.

Suppose it becomes clear that either spouse has been abused. In that case, it is necessary to immediately slow everything down and engage in an open conversation, without blame or pressure, before continuing with the intimate moment. Safety and mindfulness are vital to future engaged sexual moments. If the couple can create a loving and secure environment for communication, accepting each other as they are when they come to the relationship, while working together, they can return to the desired sexual activities that were interrupted. Many couples will benefit from counseling with a trauma-specific trained therapist or coach.

Self-Pleasuring

Some men or women worry if a history of non-addictive masturbation will affect their sexual relations in marriage. It should not, but be aware of your own personal feelings about it. If you are concerned or have any shame regarding masturbation in the past, bring it to light and discuss it with your spouse. Keep your lines of communication open.

As a couple, you may enjoy touching and pleasuring yourself during your sexual encounter. Include your spouse in any self-stimulation you might engage in. Be cautious of any sexual acts in isolation, and communicate with your spouse if it does occur. Marriage is about getting to know each other's most private intimacies and putting each other's needs first.

Vibrators and Sex Toys

The bride's girlfriends often throw a wedding shower, giving her crazy and fun gifts. The question I would always receive was about the safety of these gifts.

Using a vibrator can help a woman achieve orgasm. These can be back massagers or other types of vibrators, or you can find genital vibrators online and in stores. Some women have shared with me in my clinic that using a vibrator is a lifesaver, and they love using them as this is the only way they can orgasm.

Some women can become overstimulated with a vibrator, as it can make her almost become numb, making orgasm difficult or impossible from the clitoris being rubbed too hard for too long. Usually, stopping for a while will allow this numbing to dissipate and resolve itself.

Some women start using a vibrator with their first sexual encounter with their spouse and then continue thereafter. These women share that its use has become necessary to orgasm. These women confide that when they were newlyweds, they wished that their husbands had tried harder to learn how to arouse them with other types of foreplay before trying a vibrator. Some share that they think their husbands like to use the vibrator because they have become lazy and it is easier for them. They feel that their creativity is less than it was before. Though this is not always the case, these women's thoughts are valid. When first married, I strongly suggest that you first spend time experimenting and exploring without a vibrator, so that you can get to know each other's bodies and pleasures without assistance. You can always add these aides in later.

If you choose to try sex toys, first determine that they are not physically harmful. Do not use them as a substitute for intimacies between the two of you. Make sure that both of you are comfortable with their use. Always ask the question, "Does this behavior bring me

closer to my spouse, or does it interfere with our connection to each other?"

Scheduled Sex

Spontaneous sexual relations should be welcome
and should continue throughout your life together.
Sometimes, you can get so busy after marriage and
children that sex can become less frequent. This can be
a problem.

Though scheduling time for a sexual encounter can
sound like a chore, in reality, it can be the opposite.
The mind is suggestive, and as I mentioned earlier, *the
more you think about sex, the more you will want to have
sexual relations, and the more you have sexual relations,
the more you will think about sex*. Scheduling a set-apart
time for your sexual encounter helps you to anticipate
and think about it more. Sometimes leaving home and
getting away where you know sex will be a part of the
retreat, along with time to walk and talk together, can
help keep your marriage alive and well.

Discussing how often you would like to engage in
sex allows you to understand the sexual needs of your
spouse. Keep your lines of communication open about

this, and know that both of your sexual needs will fluctuate over time.

Fantasies

Having sexual fantasies about each other and thinking and dwelling on what sexual relations you have had in the past or will be having in the future is totally normal. In fact, it is great when you spend time dreaming about and anticipating what you might do together, hoping for many more successful sexual encounters soon.

Be safe for your spouse to share their fantasies with you. Be aware that just because a thought is shared doesn't mean that they want it actually to happen. Some couples imagine fantasy encounters with each other, or like to fantasize about back when they were dating or engaged. Fantasizing can keep a woman focused on the sexual encounter if her mind happens to wander back to folding the clothes and doing the dishes. For men, it can help them with an erection when needed. Calling each other during the day to briefly share your thoughts and fantasies about each other helps keep your spouse's sexual thoughts and desires more prevalent and can even be considered very early foreplay.

During fantasies, it is a good idea to focus your thoughts on and about each other. Avoid including other people in your fantasies. You want to keep bonding and building your sexual relationship between just the two of you as much as possible, both in your thoughts and in real life.

Mirrors, Pictures, and Videos

A patient once shared with me that she didn't feel good about her body after she had her baby until she and her husband stayed at a hotel that happened to have mirrored closet doors across from the bed. She said it changed how she felt about herself. She was pleasantly surprised to discover how beautiful she really was and how sexual she looked while making love.

Some couples like to take sexual pictures and videos of each other. However, these images are hard to delete from your camera or phone. Shy away from taking pictures of anything that you wouldn't want to show up as a surprise in an unexpected place for anyone to see. You would not want anyone else "participating" in your private relations unbeknownst to you. Also, time has a way of changing perceptions and situations.

Options might include one of the private apps that you can purchase that claim to be encrypted and secure, though I cannot verify the security of these apps. Arguably, even this information is being stored somewhere, somehow. The safest option might be visualizing yourselves having sex, watching it happen in your mind while describing it to each other, or using mirrors.

Considerations, Facts, and Choices

There are sexual options that husbands and wives can be curious about and should discuss openly. These conversations are good, as they clarify feelings about participating sexually according to your personal beliefs and respecting one another. As you consider these options, here are information and facts to consider.

Regarding Oral/Genital Sexual Relations

Benefits include:
- Potential enjoyment. Many believe that if you kiss each other on the mouth and other parts of your body, such as the neck, breasts, and abdomen, it would also feel nice to have all

your other erogenous areas kissed, including your genitals.

- Because the tongue and lips are softer than the hand or fingers, it can be a gentler foreplay measure.
- It helps women get the vagina wet and lubricated.
- If a woman struggles to have an orgasm, sometimes this is the only way a woman can become aroused and climax.
- If a man cannot continue intercourse very long without ejaculating, he can pull out and bring her to orgasm this way.
- It can help men who have a difficult time getting an erection to get firm enough to be able to enter her vagina.

Concerns include:
- Because of natural odors, a bath or shower may be advisable before participating in oral/genital relations. However, many men associate the natural fragrance of their wife arousing, as he associates that smell with sexual relations with her. Ask your spouse their preference, but also

do what is comfortable for you to be able to let go and enjoy.

- Herpes could be transmitted to the genitals if active cold sores or canker sores are in the mouth.
- The HPV (Human Papillomavirus) could be transmitted to the mouth from the genitals if infected.

As a general guideline: Avoid kissing on the mouth or engaging in oral/genital sex when sick or if you have any sores or lesions present. Transmission can occur during either oral-to-oral or oral-to-genital kissing.

Regarding Anal Intercourse

Some couples use her anus as the receptacle for his penis as an option. In my clinic, patients have voiced significant concerns to me about this.

Concerns include:

- Women report feeling left out.
- It can cause loosening of her anus.
- It can cause incontinence or leaking of feces or gas.

- It can cause or increase her hemorrhoids.
- It can tear the lining of the rectum.
- There are infection risks for both her and him.
- An absolute cleansing is necessary.
- Severe vaginal infections can occur with penetration of the vagina after anal penetration.

I have cared for thousands of women throughout my career. Of those, only a small percentage have confided that they have participated regularly in anal intercourse. Almost all have shared with me that they did not like it, and only a few have expressed that they found pleasure from anal intercourse. Some have shared that they have experimented with light touching in the anal area, and some enjoy this, but others do not. All this needs discussion. It never goes well to shock your spouse with touching in the anal area during lovemaking unless they are prepared to try it out.

Contrary to what the mainstream "how-to" books seem to promote, and as viewed on pornography, most women's perspectives in my clinic have voiced they have no desire to participate in anal intercourse. They think it is an "out hole only"—for the use of defecation purposes. Some women feel that their husbands have tried to push this form of sexual expression on them. The wives participate because they love their husbands and want to please, but they also express that they feel degraded, don't like how it feels, or feel empty when not using and enjoying their own unique female organs.

One woman whose husband kept harassing her about it finally said, "Okay, if that is what you want, then I get to stick a broomstick handle inside you first to see how it feels." She related that, after she told him that, he never asked her about it again!

Based on my experience with thousands of women, you are normal if you do not want to participate in anal intercourse. I want you to know that those feelings are valid. You can say no knowing that you are in the company of most women.

Regarding Sex During Menses

Women have asked about whether it is all right to have sex during their period (menses) and if they can get pregnant during this time. Yes, it is fine to engage in sex during this time, but it is possible to conceive even while bleeding or spotting, unless you are on birth control. A woman ovulates between twelve and sixteen (usually fourteen) days before her menses starts. She never knows for sure when that will be, so always use protection. If she uses "The Pill," IUDs, or any birth control methods that I discuss in this book as directed, she should not get pregnant while on her menses.

Having intercourse while she is on her period does not cause any safety problems for women. A few women like having sexual relations during their menses as they feel they have an increased desire or feel that their orgasms are better. However, most women and men prefer not to. One reason is the messiness of the bleeding. Of more concern is the possibility of uterine tenderness or cramping caused by deep thrusting of his penis inside her.

There are some cultures and religions where it is very taboo to have intercourse while vaginal blood is present. It is considered to be a time when a woman is alone and takes care of herself. A man is not permitted to approach his wife sexually until all bleeding is gone. It is important to talk about cultural expectations or differing backgrounds, so that you can be on the same page with each other.

Having intercourse during menses is totally up to her comfort and desires. If she does decide to go ahead, be ready with a towel underneath her (to wash easily afterward) to protect the bed or area being used, or some couples have relations in the shower for easier cleanup.

Privacy and Trust

Keep some fundamental privacy rules regarding your marriage and sex life. Not doing so can create distrust and break down your relationship.

Two major rules are:
- Don't talk to friends about your sex life, and
- Don't complain about your husband or wife to your friends.

You mustn't make light of your sexual relationship with others. What you do and how you respond during your sexual relationship is between just the two of you. Even counseling a couple almost infringes on something private—something that only you share. Your sexual encounter is unique to you. It is not a tennis match with bystanders. It is not open for a theoretical thumbs up or thumbs down emoji or community comments.

If you are having trouble talking to each other, first reread this book. If you are still having trouble, find more books to guide you through your problems. You could also find a sex therapist, counselor, medical provider, or a pastor or similar clergy member. Though I caution you to be careful, it could also be a trusted parent, sibling, or friend (one only, if possible) to help you work out and understand your problems.

With any person you approach, make sure that they know something about the sexual process. Don't assume that, just because they are older, experienced, or even in a medical position, that they know much about sexual relations and are willing to talk about it. Everyone has their own opinions. They may have a great sex life or a horrible sex life with a sexually unfulfilled spouse. Choose carefully, or it could do more damage than good.

To emphasize, the most necessary of all is talking and discussing any concerns with each other. These conversations should be first and foremost. Most issues can be resolved with open, caring, and honest communication.

6

PREVENTATIVE HEALTH FOR WOMEN

Things to consider doing now for your honeymoon and ongoing.

Should I Stretch My Hymen?

Young, virginal couples have asked me, "Can you explain the slang term *pop her cherry*?" This term refers to the bleeding (usually just a light spotting) which can occur with the first act of intercourse. Couples have been confused about the "cherry," mistakenly thinking that there is a round, red part of the female anatomy inside the vagina somewhere. There is no such anatomy—this bleeding is her actual hymenal ring, either stretching or tearing. Bleeding does not occur universally. Though not necessary for everyone, some women desire to stretch the hymenal ring before marriage. Stretching one's hymen ahead of time typically prevents her from any form of bleeding and pain. (Please refer to Figure 3 and Figure 4 of "Purpose of the Hymen" in chapter three.)

Obviously, women have been having intercourse since the beginning of time without doing this. So, how does a woman determine if she wants to stretch herself ahead of time? Some women, though not having actual intercourse, may have had some type of sexual relations involving touching of the genitals. They may have already had several of his or her own fingers introduced into the vagina repeatedly, so the hymen has been partially stretched. When intercourse does occur—and if aroused—there is not much of the hymenal ring left to open.

However, there have been times when this was not the case in my many years of practice. Couples married for weeks to years were unable to consummate their marriage by having intercourse because of her hymen being too painful to tear or stretch open. Typically, a man can see that it is painful for his new wife, so he backs off with respect. If this happens repeatedly, both of them are afraid to try any further. Other times, though he can penetrate through the hymenal ring completely, the pain and trauma of her wedding night may inhibit her process of *abandoning oneself* to become aroused. Due to this fear, her vagina never lubricates naturally nor lengthens and opens as it needs to for pleasurable intercourse. These couples are frustrated and are so grateful for help when this inhibition occurs.

Stretching the Hymen

If you desire to stretch your hymen yourself, it is simple for most women to do. If you have been able to wear a tampon without problems, or if you can insert your entire baby finger into your vagina, you should be able to stretch your hymen using your fingers. Using over-the-counter sexual lubrication, use first one finger, then two, then eventually three fingers inserted all the way into your vagina. Stretch by pulling gently to each side, then forward and back. Some discomfort or even pain can occur, but you will not harm yourself. Don't be afraid; it is not hard to do. Some women worry that they are masturbating when stretching, but you are not. It is typically not a sexual or pleasant experience.

You may find that stretching the hymen is much easier if you attempt to do this after being with your fiancé. You may notice that you are already wet and slippery because of being aroused after kissing or being near him. At that point, your vagina is more open, and it will be easier for you to try and stretch your hymen.

Stretching will only take a few minutes. If done once or twice a day, it will usually take anywhere between one stretching to a few weeks of stretching, depending on how vigorous and motivated you are. A good time is before you shower so you can wash up afterward.

Some women are nervous about touching themselves. In this case, you can use a tapered single vaginal dilator. Using lubrication, start by using the tip of the dilator. Push gently but consistently inward towards the small of your back. Most virginal women will begin to feel some pain, especially if tampons have never been used. That is okay. Push as far as you are willing to, hold it there for about ten to fifteen seconds, and push a little further if possible. Then work on it again later. You will know you have stretched the hymen sufficiently when you can insert the dilator about halfway in and can progress the dilator further into the vagina without incurring any increase in pain. Rarely, you may encounter mild bleeding, which is normal.

If you would rather wait for your honeymoon and have your husband stretch for you, allow for plenty of time to get wet and aroused. You can use an extra lubricating product if needed. My concern is for the virginal woman who premaritally has not had anything inside her vagina. Many women have related that it put a damper on their initial sexual encounter. For some women, it affected them negatively for a long time, even years.

When to See a Medical Provider

If you cannot wear tampons or insert your baby finger into your vagina, find a provider willing to discuss these things with you. They can examine you with a gentle, one-finger pelvic exam and tell you if you have any rare abnormalities of the hymen or not. Extremely rare is an imperforate hymen. This is where the hymenal ring is thicker than usual and doesn't stretch open easily, or it has an abnormally small opening, where the penis or a finger is unable to penetrate further into the vagina. Your provider will be able to tell you if you have either of these. If you do, it is resolved easily with a minor procedure from a gynecologist. I have encountered women whose hymens were as small as a pinhole opening where inserting anything into the vagina is impossible - discovering this before your honeymoon would be consequential.

Establishing a pre-sexual-activity health visit and ongoing care with a health provider is helpful as it also addresses any questions or concerns you might have about your health, birth control if desired, or regarding pre-conception. Be aware that each medical provider has their personal sexual or marriage experience and may, or may not, be comfortable with this subject matter. Medical, nursing, and midwifery school training courses all teach a variety of approaches to this subject. Your provider's comfort level and values will also influence how they approach this subject with you.

Pain with Intercourse

Most of the time, you can resolve pain with intercourse with some education. It is usually from the lack of arousal state, for whatever reason, and by not giving enough time and foreplay to allow the vagina to get ready for penile entry. During arousal, a woman's vagina opens and lengthens in preparation for him to enter her. It also becomes very slippery and wet. This must occur, or lubrication will be needed (see "Vaginal Health" in chapter six). If not, sex can be painful for a woman.

If a woman fears the pain she experienced from a previous experience with intercourse, it may be hard for her to let go and get sexually aroused. Most of the time, this fear could be from an initial or current tight hymenal ring, dryness, not enough foreplay, uncomfortable positions, or trauma. Therefore, enough time must be given to foreplay, ensuring she is more than ready for him to enter her. She will determine when that time is - just ask her. If there has been a history of trauma, talk openly about it with each other, but getting help from a therapist may be needed (see chapter five's section "History of Sexual Abuse").

Another common question a woman will ask is, "Why does intercourse hurt me in certain positions, but not always?" This tenderness can simply be the penis hitting a tender area during different times of a woman's menstrual cycle; most commonly, the cervix. Nothing is wrong in this case; and, usually, changing positions will resolve this.

Once a woman is aroused and adjusts her position as needed, it is unlikely the pain will continue. Adding in extra lubrication, even when sexually stimulated, can sometimes be helpful. If the pain persists, she needs to see her gynecology provider and evaluate if vaginal or other issues, such as vaginismus (spasms of the vagina), are present.

Urinary Tract Health (Avoiding Honeymoon Cystitis / Bladder Infections)

Here is a copy of the second sticky note that I give to my patients:

Honeymoon Helps

MEDICAL PRESCRIPTION FORM

Patient Name _____   Date _____

Address _____   Age _____

R̴X   *Honeymoon Helps*

    Cranberry Pills

    Empty bladder before and after sex

    Personal lubricants – only as needed

    Coconu, KY Natural or similar – no scent

    Rinse

    No douching

DISPENSE AS WRITTEN _____ MD

REFILL DIRECTIONS

                       DEA NO. _____

The first two items on this list:

- Cranberry pills (use them for one week before the wedding and for two to four weeks following the wedding).
- Empty your bladder before and after sex.

Why cranberry pills? There is a common type of bacteria that lives in the vaginal and perineal area that has an aversion to the properties of cranberry.

Cranberry does not treat a urinary tract infection, but it can discourage the bacteria from entering or staying in the bladder. To explain simply, the bacteria start their climb up the woman's short urethra, to reach the bladder—a nice warm comfy place to grow and set up house. These annoying bacteria find the bladder coated with cranberry. Since they don't like the cranberry, they decide to turn around and go back the way that they started to come in. The cranberry properties "offend" them. Drinking plenty of water and urinating flushes the urethra with cranberry-treated urine and usually finishes off these invading bacteria.

I suggest cranberry pills versus cranberry juice because drinking juice invites lots of calories and natural sugar in which bacteria thrives. Also, it would take many glasses of cranberry juice to equal the amount of cranberry found in most capsules or pills. If pills are not available, cranberry juice can still be helpful, as will increasing your water intake.

Though it is helpful to flush out the invading bacteria with cranberry and plenty of fluids, there will be times when she can't use the bathroom after sexual relations because of location or situation. That is okay. People have been having intercourse without cranberry pills for a long, long time. After her urethra gets used to the rubbing of intercourse, it will be more resilient and less likely to allow the bacteria to enter.

Occasionally these bacteria are not deterred, and she may need an antibiotic. Usually, the prescription medication Macrobid (Nitrofurantoin) does the trick, and a medical provider can culture her urine before treating her if necessary. If you think you have a bladder (urinary tract) infection, it is best to call your provider for treatment.

You may have only one or all of the signs and symptoms of a urinary tract infection. Typical symptoms include:

- Burning when you urinate.
- Pain when you urinate.
- Strong urge to urinate.
- The need to urinate frequently.
- Minimal amounts of urine when you do try to urinate.
- Blood in your urine.

You may have periodic pauses in your sexual activity, such as when separated from your spouse during military service. The increase in sexual activity when you get back together again can result in a bladder infection. It can be helpful to use cranberry pills again before and during the reuniting phase of your relationship.

Also, the practice of emptying your bladder before and after intercourse promotes healthy, ongoing bladder care throughout your life.

Vaginal Health

Sometimes, for no apparent reason, or when you engage in a sexual encounter multiple times within a day, a woman cannot produce the natural vaginal lubricants that the body usually provides. No matter how aroused you are, you may not secrete the moisture needed for penile entry. This lack of secretions is also usual for some women, even when sexually aroused. This is when you should use personal lubricants.

For example, you may be on your honeymoon at the ocean, where you are out in the sun and saltwater all day. You had intercourse that morning before spending the rest of the day at the beach. That evening, you want to have intercourse again. You feel sexually excited, but you find that you cannot get wet enough for him to enter you no matter what you try. You have become dehydrated and need more fluids in your body to produce vaginal lubrication. Over-the-counter sexual lubrication may be helpful in this case.

Use as natural a lubricant as possible. Make sure to avoid any lubricant that is labeled erotic, tingling, flavored, scented, or sensational in any way. These enhanced lubricants often have perfumes and oils as one of their ingredients. These ingredients may cause you to react with inflammation of the sensitive and soft mucous membranes of the vulva and vaginal opening, thus causing burning, redness, or even an allergic reaction. Also, if condoms are involved, make sure to use a water-based lubricant, as other types of over-the-counter lubricants can affect or break down the condom and its effectiveness in preventing pregnancy.

Lack of natural vaginal lubrication can be for a variety of reasons:
- It's normal for some bodies,
- Lack of hydration (not enough water in your diet),
- Dehydration from the sun,
- Dehydration from saltwater,
- Frequent intercourse with orgasm (some

women will not become as aroused and lubricated because their sexual needs have recently been met),

- Decreased estrogen hormone can decrease libido and vaginal secretions,
- Breastfeeding (dehydration from not drinking enough water for both yourself and the milk you produce for your baby), or
- Menopause.

Some women have reactions to all lubricants and feel these lubricants contribute to vaginal irritation, recurring yeast infections, or a bacterial infection. As an alternative, a simple and natural way to add moisture, is to use her own or her husband's saliva and place it on the vulvar lips and vaginal opening. This wetness can help to start foreplay. Don't do this if either the woman or man is sick with a respiratory infection, contagious disease, herpes cold sore, any lesion, chancre, or other concern she might have regarding her mouth or lips. Some couples also use oral/genital relations as a way to lubricate with saliva.

If he tries to enter the vagina when she is too dry, her vagina can get irritated, with small micro-cracks developing, causing a place for yeast to grow. Ensuring the vagina is wet and slippery before any entry occurs helps prevent this from happening.

If she does start to feel itchy and raw in the vaginal and vulvar area, and she thinks she has an overgrowth of yeast in her vagina, she can try an over-the-counter Monistat or generic vaginal yeast cream. However, be aware that without a diagnosis by a medical provider, it is hard to know if this is the correct diagnosis of the problem. Always contact your provider for advice and treatment.

Suppose her vagina becomes rubbed a little raw from "overuse" without any itching or signs of a yeast infection. In that case, she can use a non-scented oil such as Vaseline®, shortening, coconut oil, olive oil, or shea butter after she rinses off or bathes her genitals. Some of these may not work as well when used as sexual lubricants but can be applied to the vulvar area after the rubbing that occurs during sexual relations to help protect and soothe any irritation.

Odors

Healthy vaginal secretions do not have an unpleasant smell. The opposite is true, as most men find the scent of an aroused vagina to be sexually stimulating. However, these same secretions can develop an unpleasant smell once they contact the air for a while. As the day goes on, some odor may develop in the genital area. This smell is easily cared for with a shower, bath, or even when using a bidet. I recommend general good hygiene with a daily shower or whenever this odor becomes noticeable. Some women and men like to shower or rinse their genitals before starting the sexual encounter, especially if they anticipate engaging in oral/genital relations. However, as discussed earlier in the book, some men find their wife's genital odor arousing even when it is bothersome to her. You can simply ask each other.

Occasionally during my practice, a woman would call complaining of a bad smell originating from her vagina. Before making her come in for an appointment, I would ask her to take a good shower or bath, and right when finished, put one finger in her vagina and then test the smell. If it had a foul odor, then she needed to come in; but if not, she was fine. It may mean that she only needs to rinse her genitals or shower more often.

No Douching!

Douching uses water or a preparation bought over the counter to "clean out" the vagina. It is an old-fashioned routine of some older women after intercourse who thought that it would flush out any semen and generally keep their vagina clean. However, the opposite is what occurs! The beneficial flora/bacteria found in the vagina naturally keep the vagina's PH and floral balance just the way that they should be. A foul-smelling infection named bacterial vaginosis can be a result of douching. Don't use a douche unless prescribed on a rare occasion by your medical provider. Simply washing or rinsing off the entire genital area will eliminate any fluids or odor.

Birth Control

Do you desire to prevent pregnancy when first married? If yes, seeing a gynecological medical provider such as a nurse midwife, OB/GYN physician, nurse practitioner, family practice physician, or physician assistant is needed. Any of these providers should give counsel and provide any birth control option.

The discussion below does not include any review of the risk factors, contraindication, or list all possible side effects from using these contraceptive methods. I've kept to the basic information for quick reading. Your medical provider will need to talk about the indications for use, risks, how it works, and side effects of any birth control method. This text is just a brief overview of the most common pros and cons of birth control that women have shared with me throughout the years of my practice.

Below are methods of birth control that are available currently that I recommend. Some affect a woman's menses, some her mood, some do not affect her at all, but all will effectively prevent pregnancy, if used as directed.

It is not true that she needs more than one birth control method unless she uses one of the more unreliable methods or takes the drug Accutane or other teratogenic (fetal harming) drugs. Also, some people believe that she needs to be on birth control for many months for effectiveness. This belief is also not true. Most birth control methods will require starting when her period starts each month or starting a few weeks before her first act of intercourse. The prescribing provider will know.

Couples often have questions about how each birth control method prevents pregnancy. I briefly address those questions here.

Many couples have concerns about when life begins and whether a birth control method works by "terminating" pregnancy. The birth control methods I have listed below do not work in this manner. They mostly work by preventing the egg and sperm from meeting. I say "mostly" because there can always be some unknown factors contributing in a way that we cannot study. I have presented the choices in the most transparent way possible.

"The Pill"

The combination oral contraceptive pill, or "The Pill" (many brand and generic names) is a simple birth control option to try first because it is easy to start and discontinue. It is a combination of both estrogen and progestin. It prevents pregnancy mainly by suppressing the woman from ovulating (not allowing the egg to release) and thickening cervical mucous, which blocks the sperm from entering the uterus. It does not have any ill effect on her future ability to get pregnant. It is possible to get pregnant immediately after quitting The Pill.

Some of the possible side effects of The Pill are both positive and negative. With all of these birth control methods, the information below includes only the main side effects that some women experience and report to me consistently.

Positive side effects of The Pill:

- It regulates her period, so she knows when it is going to start.
- It lightens her flow, from heavy to medium, from medium to light, or from light to no periods at all. It is not a problem if periods are completely absent while on The Pill.
- It can decrease pain from menstrual cramps.
- It is easy to start up and discontinue use.
- It helps women with insulin resistance such as polycystic ovarian syndrome (PCOS).
- It can help with acne.

- It can help improve mood swings and anxiety, though sometimes it can make this worse, depending on the specific type of The Pill.
- It decreases fear about getting pregnant, which helps with the letting go and abandoning oneself process needed for a good sexual experience.
- It prevents pregnancy approximately 98 percent of the time.

Negative side effects of The Pill:
- It can cause nausea for the first few months.
- The increased estrogen can bind with the testosterone, causing a decrease in her arousal state or sex drive.
- Her moods can be affected negatively.
- She must remember to take it daily.
- She needs a provider to prescribe it.

I want to emphasize that every woman responds uniquely to The Pill. If you, as a husband, notice a negative effect on her mood or libido after she starts birth control, please encourage her to address this with her provider. If she is unhappy with The Pill, it is easy to move to the other birth control options, such as the IUDs or progestin implants, which require insertion by a medical provider.

Intrauterine Device (IUD)

There are two main types of Intrauterine Devices (IUD):
- Copper hormone-free IUD, and
- Progestin-only IUD.

IUDs are excellent for women who don't want to take a pill daily. Both are considered 99 percent effective. A medical provider places the IUD inside the uterus during an office visit. It is a fast and simple procedure but can cause some temporary discomfort. Your medical provider can counsel which IUD would be the best option.

The Copper IUD

ParaGard is the brand name for the copper IUD. If she has a light to medium menstrual cycle to start with, the copper IUD can be a good option. The copper

IUD discourages fertilization. It is wrapped with small amounts of copper ions that:

- Create inflammation inside the uterus.
- Cause the cervical opening to be blocked by a spermicidal mucous, stopping most of the sperm from entering into the uterus.
- Attract and slow the swimming of the sperm, keeping it away from the egg.
- Cause the women's white blood cells to target all foreign cells, including sperm.

Positive aspects of the copper IUD are:
- No hormonal side effects.
- Most economical for the long term.
- Lasts for ten years, unless she desires removal sooner.
- No effect or delay in fertility when removed.
- 99 percent effective against pregnancy.

Adverse aspects of the copper IUD are:
- An increase in menstrual flow—if she has a heavy menses to start with, it may not be the best option, though your provider can help you decide.

- An increase in cramping—if she already experiences severe cramping, she should consider another birth control option.
- If pregnancy does occur (approximately 1 percent chance), it is more likely to be an ectopic pregnancy than with the other forms of birth control. (Remember that you only have a 1 percent chance of pregnancy and then only a slight chance of it being ectopic.) Women can carry a baby to term with the copper IUD inside them if a pregnancy occurs, but the pregnancy will require closer monitoring.

The progestin-only IUD

The current names available at the time of this publication are: Liletta, Skyla, Mirena, and Kyleena.

The progestin-only IUD:
- Is helpful for women who want to avoid the use of any estrogen in their birth control method.
- Usually lightens menses, or menses become absent.
- Is sometimes used to treat severe menstrual problems.

- Has manufacturer's package instructions that state that, after six months, there is no difference in fertility between the progestin-only IUDs and other birth control methods.
- Is 99 percent effective against pregnancy.
- Lasts three to seven years, depending on the brand used.

The possible side effects of the progestin-only IUD are all very similar. They are listed below under "Progestin-Only Birth Control Methods."

Progestin-Only Birth Control Methods

Progestins work by:
- Discouraging ovulation.
- Increasing cervical mucous, which blocks the entry of the sperm into the uterus.
- Thinning out the uterine lining, creating a hostile environment where the sperm can't reach the egg.

Because of this thinning of the uterine lining with progestin-only birth control methods, there is some thought by concerned women that this thin lining might prevent implantation of the zygote (five-days-old fertilized egg). While medical experts cannot say with 100 percent certainty that this does not occur, most medical professionals consider that the prevention of pregnancy occurs by the first three mechanisms discussed—no ovulation; cervical mucous blocking the sperm from entering the uterus; from a generally hostile environment preventing the sperm and egg from uniting. In support of this, women can still get pregnant with any progestin-only birth control methods and carry their baby to a healthy delivery.

Here is a list of the progestin-only birth control methods:

- Liletta, Mirena, etc.—the progestin-only IUDs (discussed above),
- Nexplanon—the arm implant,
- "Mini Pill" (many brand and generic names)—the progestin-only (no estrogen) birth control pill, and
- Depo-Provera injection.

Positive aspects of progestin-only birth control methods include:

- No estrogen side effects.
- Usually, lightening of menses.
- A decrease in menstrual cramps.

Negative aspects of the progestin-only birth control methods include:

- Irregular vaginal spotting and bleeding, sometimes with or without menses. (Some women spot every day, while other women quit bleeding altogether, with no menses at all.)
- Almost always, you will have some type of change in your menses.
- Though not reported in the literature, I have heard some women express feeling that it contributed to a decrease in their sex drive.
- Some increase in vaginal irritation or infections because of the ongoing menstrual spotting (if this side effect occurs).

Progestin-only arm implant

Nexplanon is a thin, flexible arm implant placed just under the skin of the non-dominant upper arm by a healthcare provider. It is inserted at the office, as a minor procedure, with very minimal pain. It avoids the discomfort of an IUD insertion but with the same benefits. It also:

- Is a good choice for women who do not want any estrogen in their birth control.
- Is suitable for those that don't want to remember to take a pill daily.
- Can last for three years, unless you want to take it out sooner.
- Is 99 percent effective.
- Is recommended for young teens or someone who isn't comfortable with an IUD insertion.

The "Mini Pill"—progestin-only birth control pill

The *Mini Pill* is a progestin-only pill without the ingredient of estrogen like *The Combination Pill* has in it. It doesn't have estrogen; nothing is inserted into her body; it does not require removal when finished with use. It is a suitable option for someone who wants a reasonably good method of birth control. It also:

- Is commonly used for women while breastfeeding, as there is some thought that the estrogen in The Pill can decrease milk supply, and the progestin-only Mini Pill has no estrogen in it.
- Must be taken at the same time each day (if more than three hours later taking it each day, the risk of pregnancy increases).
- Is only 94 percent effective, if used perfectly.
- Causes irregular spotting or change in menses similar to other progestin-only birth control methods.

Other Mini Pill side effects are listed above under "Progestin-Only Birth Control Methods."

Depo-Provera injection

The Depo-Provera injection is a "shot" into her muscle that will last for about three months. When using Depo-Provera for birth control:

- She must receive the injection every twelve weeks.
- It is 99 percent effective in preventing pregnancy.

- Abnormal vaginal bleeding and spotting can sometimes increase with the first injection; but, after the second or more injections, menses usually go away completely.
- Menstrual problems become less severe, or some women choose to use it when they don't want to have any periods at all.
- There can be a delay of up to one year of return to fertility after discontinuation of use.
- It has possible bone loss if used long term, though the bone density returns to normal after discontinuation.

Condoms

A condom, if used correctly, is 98 percent effective and works by preventing fertilization. Quite a few couples in my practice prefer using condoms for their birth control method. They are easy to find in any drug store. Many couples use condoms as a sexy part of foreplay or lovemaking—have fun with it!

You must use a condom correctly. Important instructions are:

- It must cover the penis the entire time, not just before ejaculation. A fluid secreted from the penis as pre-lubricant semen contains sperm. It is unknown exactly when this pre-lubricant semen is going to occur.
- You should not begin intercourse without a condom, and then pull out to put the condom on immediately before ejaculation, or else pregnancy can occur from the pre-lubricant semen.
- The penis must be removed from the vagina soon after ejaculation to prevent leakage. Hold the condom at the base of the penis to prevent it from sliding off and potentially allowing semen to run into the vagina.
- Make sure that she is well lubricated (naturally or with a water-based lubricant), or else the condom could tear.

Not doing these practices can result in pregnancy, and I have seen many pregnancies occur from not using condoms properly. When I asked these couples for more details, 100 percent of the time, somebody missed at least one of the practices discussed above.

Positive aspects of condom use are:

- No hormonal side effects.
- They are readily available without a prescription.
- The prevention of some sexually transmitted diseases.
- A decrease in the "mess" of intercourse.
- Some women who have hypersensitivity to semen like using condoms.

Adverse aspects of condom use are:

- A possible increase in the cost of birth control if having sex frequently due to purchasing a larger quantity of condoms.
- If either person is allergic to latex, they must use lambskin condoms (more expensive).
- Have the potential to break.
- Hinders spontaneity if you don't have a condom with you.
- May decrease sexual sensations for both the man and woman.

If you don't know which method sounds best, you can try one of the above birth control methods and see how it works for you and your spouse. Switching to using condoms is always an option if nothing else is working for you, or if you prefer them.

Other Methods of Birth Control

There are a few other methods of birth control that I have not discussed. These are the diaphragm, cervical cap, the female condom, the withdrawal method (pull out), and natural family planning (the rhythm method, which is based on her menses schedule and other signs of ovulation). They all work by preventing or avoiding fertilization. However, they are not as effective or convenient as the other types of birth control discussed above.

7

A LASTING MARRIAGE

Maintaining your relationship in marriage, both sexual and otherwise, is kind of like servicing a car. Keeping your car waxed and polished keeps it looking beautiful and will help keep the paint job from fading. With a new, well-maintained vehicle, you can drive it for quite a while without problems. However, eventually, it must be cared for and serviced. If not, it will ultimately break down and you will need to replace it. You do not want this to happen to your marriage! Being attentive about keeping your relationship "polished" and "tuned up" will keep both your marriage and its sexual relations running smoothly.

My saying, *service is the spice of life,* is true in many ways. Serving your spouse brings connection, depth, and meaning to relationships. Doing nice things, being attentive to one another, and caring about each other's desires will continually build, reinforce, or create an even stronger connection between the two of you.

This thought reminds me of a moment many years ago that represents this concept. Not long after our first daughter was born, Greg and I were excited to purchase an older, standard-tract home built in the 1950s. Though not fancy, it was in a quiet, friendly neighborhood. My younger brother, Mat, had just transferred to attend the local university and lived in our basement. He was independent, definitely single, and never had much to do with our baby girl.

One day I needed a sitter desperately. He reluctantly agreed to tend our four-month-old daughter, and I left him careful instructions on what to feed her and how to care for her, and then I ran out the door.

When I returned, he was holding her in his arms. "How was she?" I asked tentatively. He didn't respond right away; instead, he sighed, "I fell in love with my niece today." He was looking down at her with the sweetest expression. Curious and a bit surprised, I asked, "Why, what happened?" With conviction, he responded, "It happened when I was feeding her. She was crying when I picked her up. I was a little scared that I wouldn't know how to help her. I gave her the bottle, and she initially kind of played with it, just looking like she didn't know quite what to make of me, but at least she had quit crying, which was good. I was worried that she wouldn't take it, so I talked with her and told her she needed to eat while I wiggled the bottle. After a moment, she smiled at me, and a little milk started dribbling out of the side of her mouth. Then she got serious and started gobbling it up. She stared at me super intensely the whole time she ate." As he gently cuddled her, rocking, he said, "There was something about picking her up, helping her to eat, and caring for her. I know it sounds crazy, but while I was feeding her, all of a sudden, I felt so much love for her!"

I smiled and loved it!

This story is the perfect example of what can happen when you care for and give service to someone—you create a bond that would not have existed before. The recipient also connects with you, grateful for the service that you've given or the exchange between you. So, how can you "service" your relationship to keep it like it is now? We will discuss this in a moment.

Remembering Whom You Married

I have heard women express in my clinic that their marriage is not what they had envisioned. They state that their husbands no longer spend time talking to or cuddling them like they used to when they were dating, engaged, or first married.

Husbands complain that their wives don't give them the attention that they need, compared to the connection that they experienced while dating or engaged, and that they don't seem to admire them as they did before. They say that it's like their wives never want to do anything fun anymore.

I have studied and pondered these complaints and concerns and have developed a tool that will help solve this problem. We will discuss this tool in the next section, but first, I want you both to look introspectively at who you are right now. Look at the priority that you place on and how you treat one another.

If you are currently engaged or early in your marriage, then, most likely, you are "servicing" the relationship and giving to each other constantly. Think of how present you are and how much time you spend as a couple connecting with each other, such as talking or holding hands or kissing. You need this same amount of time and undivided attention after you are married to maintain and keep your marriage and sexual relationship healthy. When one of you is struggling or upset about something, right now, you are there for each other, soothing each other with love and kindness. How well a couple can self-soothe, care for each other, or be a part of comforting each other is part of the key to a healthy marriage.

For Him

There are a lot of books and advice about what you need to do to "keep your wife in love with you," such as opening the car door for her, sending her flowers, etc.— but these things aren't what most women are searching for and need. Those things are lovely, and I enjoy them when my husband does them for me. However, what you genuinely need to do to stay in love with each other are some of the same things that made you fall in love with each other in the first place!

Daily, you likely have long, meaningful conversations with her. You notice how beautiful she is and tell her often. You are mindful of her, often hold her hand, or put your arm around her when out in public. How often do you linger when you gaze at each other? These are just a few of the things that have made *her* fall in love with *you*.

Continuing to do the things that you do right now will be your guide for marriage. Write them down to remember for later, as nothing will be more apparent to you than these notes regarding what action that you should take if you find yourself drifting apart. This guide will be helpful if she seems dissatisfied, is not wanting to spend time in the activities that you enjoy, or if she doesn't want to have sexual relations with you as much as she did before.

For Her

You are most likely currently doing the things that he loves, which is why he fell in love with you. If you can remember these specific activities and do them consistently for the rest of your life, it will make a big difference in your relationship. It also goes a long way in helping him remember the woman he married.

For example, do you make an extra effort to try and look nice for him? Do you gladly participate in recreation and activities that he likes? For those of you on your way to the altar, I'm sure that you enjoy looking forward to making love with him in the future. Right now, you marvel at how handsome he is. You have confidence and trust in his decisions, admiring him for his talents and capabilities. I'm pretty sure that, at this moment, you think that he can accomplish just about anything.

Growing and changing together is a necessary and important part of marriage. However, so often after marriage, many women seem to forget that they married a very capable and self-sufficient man. Instead, they want to "fix" him. They want to tell him what to wear, how to drive, how to wear his hair, how to act, and what to do. I maintain that if you remember to treat him later like you have while dating or engaged, you will continue to have that wonderful man you married as your husband.

Don't try to change him. It is evident that right now, he can live his life without your help, just as you are capable and able to take care of yourself. He has lived it well enough that you think he is a good catch. Telling him what to do can take down his confidence, and, in reality, it is not your business to make decisions for him. Know that he thinks so highly of what you think! You need not manipulate that power. He loves that you admire him so much. Just trust him. Let him be his own boss and accomplish his own goals in life so you can continue that admiration for him. Don't try to change him. Instead, work on advancing in life together with love, consideration, and respect.

So, how to keep this? This next section discusses what I suggest to my patients.

Your Personal Guide to a Lasting Marriage

Noticing your current behaviors and recording these actions will give you the answer to the question of "How do we stay in love and keep our sex life wonderful?" *Journaling your current activities* is an effective tool for identifying a pattern to follow in the future.

This guide will be simple and easy to build, but you need to start doing it right now. I cannot stress how important this is! At the beginning of marriage, you have a completely different insight about your life and each other that you will never have again. If you are at this point in your life, please don't lose this once-in-a-lifetime perspective! Write your unique formula down now by keeping track of what you are doing and saying. Take screenshots of your texts, send them to yourself, and then place them in a journal folder. If you are not newlyweds, write down as much as you remember about dating and engagement. Do this individually, and then discuss it together to develop as complete a list as possible.

The other option (or combining both) would be to answer the questions below. Consider other thoughts that might benefit your future relationship. Doing this activity together is enjoyable as a couple.

During the course of one day to one week, right now ask yourself:

How often do I think of them?

How often do I call or text them on the phone?

What are our conversations about?

How many hours each day do we spend together?

What do we do when we are together?

What recreational activities do we do or talk about wanting to do together?

Do we share our dreams, goals, and experiences?

How often do I compliment them?

How often do I openly or privately show affection toward them?

How often do I think about kissing, holding, or anticipating having sex with them?

How often and for how long do we linger and gaze at one another, kiss, or hold each other close?

How often do I try to look nice, shower, use perfume/cologne, etc., for them?

What acts of kindness do I do for them?

When struggling or flooded with emotion about something, how often do we soothe each other?

If we have disagreements, what are they about? How do we work together to resolve them?

How often do I try to convince them about something?

How often do I try to get them to change?

How often do we agree with each other or willingly go along with each other?

How often do I give unsolicited advice?

Other thoughts or ideas:

Even if you don't like some of the answers, make as many notes as you can. After your wedding day, put these notes aside in a safe place for later use. Don't worry too much if some of the questions listed above leave you in an unfavorable position. These items may not matter to your fiancé/spouse. Just ask them and find out. If there are important things to them, you will have the opportunity to discuss them together and work on them. You may feel a sense of rejection or discouragement (if you are not doing these things well); but, by talking, you can replace these feelings with empathy for each other and hope for the future.

This guide is for your future use, to reflect introspectively, and to note how you can better contribute to your relationship. You will use it as your guide on what you—*individually*—could be doing (or not doing) to improve your marriage.

Every Six Months

Six months after your marriage, or if not feeling as connected as before, pull out this guide. See how you are doing now compared to when you first married. Recognize where you *individually* might be able to step it up or possibly back off. *Trust that your spouse will try* just as hard as you.

Also, notice and appreciate how much you both have grown. Avoid using "Your Personal Guide to a Lasting Marriage" as a weapon against each other— accusing your spouse about what they are or are not doing. Remember, you both can make changes for the better.

A caution: You want your spouse to be the best that they can be, so you want to help by giving suggestions. Though discussions are good, try not to push or make decisions for them. Instead, ask the other person what they think. That is what you did when dating and engaged, didn't you? You wanted to know their thoughts.

You tried to align yourself with them to prove that you were a good match. You might be surprised to find out they are still just as capable as when you were courting each other and can solve the problem, though differently than you, without your help.

Please remember that carving out one-on-one time for each other for connection, just like you did while dating, is of great importance! When you are super busy for different reasons, time and effort will be needed the most. Each individual's needs—as well as the needs of their spouse—may change and grow throughout their life. Still, people never stop needing to be held, hugged, loved, respected, and admired. Don't forget to do nice things for each other like you did when you first fell in love.

CONCLUDING THOUGHTS

Congratulations! The fact that you completed this book indicates that you have made it a priority to either start on a good path to a satisfying and healthy sexual relationship in your future marriage or to enrich your current one. This is an important first step, and you should feel good about your accomplishment! However, as reflected in these pages, a healthy, open, kind, and ongoing dialogue will be needed to continue moving you in the right direction.

Remember that, as a man and woman, you have been given what is needed to fulfill your role as a spouse in marriage, but some of you have not had this behavior role modeled in your life. In some manner, most of us have not developed all the essential skills. Don't be fearful of reaching and working for what you desire to be so that you will have a wonderful marriage and a fulfilling sex life. I hope that, by reading this short book, you have been able to gain better confidence in yourselves, trusting and bringing forth your feelings of love, kindness, service, and gratitude for each other while ignoring or minimizing the judging, defensive, and selfish thoughts and actions.

Please consider my counsel below. It summarizes and helps you remember what marriage requires. And, always, enjoy a wonderful rest of your lives together!

"Just like you need to service a car, spending time taking care of one another will keep your relationship running and full of gas, helping it to last a long time."

OTHER BOOKS
BY S. LAURIE HANSEN

Rock-iT Barre, Book One: Basic Guitar & Rock-iT Barre Use

Rock-iT Barre, Book Two: Advanced Method

Rock-iT Barre, Song Book One

ABOUT THE AUTHOR

Laurie Hansen, CNM, has spent over for-ty-two years helping thousands of women with their reproductive and gynecological health. She worked as a registered nurse in labor and delivery upon  graduation from Westminster College in Salt Lake City. During that time, she also specialized in high-risk antenatal testing, which led her to lecturing nationally, presenting courses in fetal monitoring, antenatal testing, RN limited ultrasound training, and second-stage labor management. Her research regarding management of the descent of the fetus in the second stage of labor was published in the well-known OB/GYN *Green Journal* and is cited in textbooks internationally.

After seventeen years of working as a registered nurse, she returned to school to obtain her master's of science in nurse-midwifery at the University of Utah and graduated in 1994. She opened the first independent, woman-owned, mid-level medical practice at the Salt Lake Clinic. Laurie has been recognized for her excellence in teaching medical students (among other awards) and has taught at the high school level in the subjects of health and health occupations.

Following the death of her first husband from cancer, she remarried. She and her five daughters moved to Southern Utah, where she opened the first nurse-midwifery OB/GYN practice, with births occurring at the local hospital. She delivered all of her twenty-six grandchildren and loves spending time with them by singing in the car, hosting "cousins camp" each year, skiing, and backpacking with them. She also likes spending time in these activities with her husband, adult children, and their spouses.

She performed in a rock 'n' roll band for over thirty years. Now she uses her musical abilities by singing and playing guitar at church and funeral services with her daughters, conducting a youth choir, and teaching her grandchildren's elementary school classes crazy and fun camp and public domain songs. The teachers and hundreds of students fondly named and call her the "Singing Grandma." She invented, sells, and owns the patent on the Rock-iT Barre Guitar and Ukulele Chording Device, which assists those with arthritis or missing digits in continuing to play the guitar.

Laurie values sharing her knowledge and experience with those interested in learning. She enjoys finding ways to serve her family, community, and church. Most importantly, she loves knowing that she is a daughter of God, who patiently helps her grow and learn.

Laurie can be reached at:

SuccessfulBookSeries@gmail.com.